LICHEN DYES
The New Source Book

Karen Diadick Casselman

DOVER PUBLICATIONS, INC.
Mineola, New York

Bibliographical Note

This Dover edition, first published in 2001, is a revised, second edition of *Lichen Dyes: A Source Book,* originally published in 1996 by Studio Vista Publications, Cheverie, Nova Scotia. Forty percent of the text has been revised for the present edition, which includes 1998 Australian research.

Library of Congress Cataloging-in-Publication Data

Casselman, Karen Leigh, 1942–
    Lichen dyes : the new source book / Karen Diadick Casselman.—2nd rev. ed.
        p. cm.
    "A revised, second edition of Lichen dyes: a source book, originally published in 1996 by Studio Vista Publications, Cheverie, Nova Scotia"—T.p. verso.
    Includes bibliographical references and indexes.
    ISBN 0-486-41231-8 (pbk.)
    1. Dyes and dyeing, Domestic. 2. Lichens. I. Title.

TT854.3 .C38 2001
667'.26—dc21

00-063882

Manufactured in the United States of America
Dover Publications, Inc., 31 East 2nd Street, Mineola, N.Y. 11501

DEDICATION

This book is dedicated to my students—from Alaska to Australia—who have taught me as much as I have taught them; and to my professors at Saint Mary's University, Halifax, where, as a mature graduate student, I received consideration and encouragement to pursue new directions in an under-studied subject field.

Contents

Dye Charts

Preface: An Ethical Approach

For at least 4,000 years, more confusion has accumulated on the subject of lichen dyes than on any other dyestuff in the history of civilization. Why is this so? Is it because lichens are mysterious plants that hold their colour potential like closely kept secrets? Misinformation and contradiction clutter the story. But research (see Bibliography) has begun to unravel the puzzle. More than 300 references have been surveyed to provide here, in a single source, information of use to both novice and experienced dyers, historians and teachers, scholars and textile writers.

Lichen dyeing is a compelling and controversial research field, which may be why these dyes are so misunderstood. Is lichen dyeing simply unethical? Do the dyes fade? Neither allegation is true. This study, based on 25 years of research, aims to separate fact and reality from fiction and folklore. Another goal is to demonstrate conservation by setting an example; to show that ethical dye formulas are possible; to offer advice on ways to utilize "found" (detached) lichens; and to include new ways to improve fastness.

Lichens make brilliant textile dyes. BWM (boiling water method) shades include yellow, orange, ochre, russet, brown, copper, bronze, olive and true green. Pink, mauve, violet, red, rose, magenta and purple are typical AM (ammonia method) colours. POD (photo-oxidized) blues are a third category described in Chart 3a, p. 26. That these colours can be enjoyed without causing damage to the environment depends upon ethical dye formulas, which in this book are based on one-tenth to one-sixteenth the volume of lichens once used (p. 26).

Lichen dyes are an education in ecology and ethics. To use lichens is to explore the point where craft and material culture intersect science and natural history. No other dyes provide a better opportunity to learn how to protect the environment: this has been the foundation of my teaching philosophy for two decades. Dyers now understand that you can remove part of a lichen without destroying it (p. 51). They know how to practice botanical "thrift" by using several lichen species in a single dye bath (pp. 26, 51). Furthermore, the Dyer's Code of Ethics (p. 47) and salvage botany

1

promote effective ways to find (rather than harvest) lichens that will be otherwise wasted or destroyed.

Lichen dyeing could survive as just one more incorrect entry in an encyclopedia, but I have chosen through my academic work to perpetuate it as a living heritage (see Epilogue). As an educator, my goal is to encourage ethical practices with regard to ecology and conservation. I would argue that, like good technique and personal safety, these issues are integral to modern craft. Developing ethical lichen dyes is one way to reclaim a misunderstood part of textile history. The richness of the narrative—and its relevance to postmodern issues such as cultural appropriation, gender and ethnicity (themes I explore in my book *The Gorsebrook Papers*)—suggest that a new interpretation is timely.

I firmly believe that those who bring passion, energy and intelligence to their textile work can also be trusted to help assure a safe future for lichens. The key to conservation is for textile dyers to become part of that solution.

NOTE: Many images relevant to this text are in my articles and previous books; a list of more than 15 years of such publications is included here on p. 56. (See also Bibliography.)

Should You Use Lichen Dyes?
Ten Questions and Answers

It takes patience and practice to learn to identify lichens before you make dyes (see Code of Ethics, p. 48). Not everyone is that serious. If you are unsure about my "learn-before-you-dye" philosophy, the following questions and answers may help you to decide.

1. *Is lichen dyeing difficult?* No, but there is a correlation between correct lichen identification (p. 50), the appropriate dye method (Chart 3a, p. 27) and satisfactory results.

2. *Do lichen dyes fade?* My lichen-dyed fibres (photographs of which may be found in many publications: see p. 57 and Bibliography) were dried in direct sunlight.

3. *What can you dye with lichens?* Fabric and fibres of wool and silk, cotton clothing, embroidery floss and knitting fibres of acrylic, nylon, orlon and rayon blends can be dyed with lichens, as can paper, plastic buttons, raffia, shells, marble, leather and basketry materials. Even food and human hair can be dyed using lichens.

4. *How do lichens actually make dyes?* Lichens contain acids, or substances that are dye precursors (p. 49). These substances are treated in one of three ways (AM, BWM or POD dyes: Chart 3a, p. 27) to form new compounds, or pigments.

5. *How many lichens are required to make a dye?* Several handfuls of "found" lichens (pp. 27, 45) will dye enough yarn to knit or weave a hat or scarf.

6. *Are mordants required?* Lichen dyes are substantive (see Glossary), so strictly speaking, no mordants are required. But "alternative" mordants (Chart 4, p. 43) are used to vary the many colours available in the AM and BWM palettes.

7. *Do lichens grow only in the wilderness?* Lichens can be found almost anywhere—even in cities. The trick is to find those already detached from their substrate (p. 51).

3

8. *What have ethics to do with lichen dyes?* Everything! Some recipes use too many lichens, and this is wasteful. The ratios used in this book (p. 26) are safer for the environment, and hence more ethical.

9. *What is salvage botany?* It is a non-exploitive way we can utilize plants and lichens that will be otherwise destroyed or wasted (pp. 26, 51).

10. *What are the chances of collecting a rare lichen by mistake?* Rare lichens, like rare birds, are most often discovered by professionals. It is no more difficult to learn five common lichen names than it is to recognize five species of birds, so familiarity is the best assurance. (And lichens don't move. Or *do* they? See Casselman 1993a, p. 172.)

1

History of Asian and Southern European Lichen Dyes

Ancient Purples

Imagine a marketplace in the Levant at the time of the Crusades. The air is redolent with spices, copper pots shimmer in the sun, and stalls are draped with sumptuous fabrics. A group of Crusaders, led by an affluent Florentine, strolls through the bazaar. The men stop to admire fabulous purple silks that glow in the inviting shade of one particular stall. The trader beckons them inside. Back in Europe, the Crusades have created a demand for Eastern textiles, and the prospect of profit is as enticing to the gentleman from Florence as are the alluring and unfamiliar purple dyes.

The man's name is Federigo, and later he returns to Italy with the orchil formula (see Glossary). The purple lichen dye makes the Florentine family so famous that eventually they adopt a surname (first spelled as "Orcellai," then "Rucellai") that becomes synonymous with purple. The fame of the Rucellai family lives on, for orchil lichens (genus *Roccella*: Chart 2a, p. 17) are named in their honour. Also perpetuated—regrettably—is the myth that Federigo "discovered" a lost tradition.

But centuries before the Crusades, Neolithic cultures had purple dyes. A remarkable woollen robe has been excavated from a Chinese burial site circa 2000 B.C. (Barber 1999) and the colour is still a beautiful reddish-purple. The excitement surrounding this—the very first entire purple garment—is heightened by a mystery involving Caucasian migration into China at such an early time. The Ürümchi garments also confirm purple dye technology in a period that pre-dates the advent of purple, at Crete. But whether these ancient garments were dyed with murex (see Glossary), kermes, or an early AM lichen dye, the Ürümchi purples confirm a technology that parallels Tyrian purple.

5

Phoenician Purples

This is where the saga of ancient lichen dyes begins, at Tyre. The visceral response to colour and the desire to be rich are not passions unique to Federigo. As "Tyrian purple" (one of many murex synonyms) implies, the Phoenicians took the credit for inventing mollusc purples. But archaeological evidence shows that shellfish dyes were made at Crete circa 2000 B.C. (Barber 1991). Myths about how purple began are consistent with a colour that invokes passion, for love is the primary ingredient in these fables. One story involves a shepherdess (Tyrus) whose dog tears apart a mollusc on the beach; predictably, the dog's snout turns purple. Similar stories abound in European folklore (Sandberg 1997). In the Greek version, the god Melkart apparently pleads with Tyrus to become his bride, for until now she has steadfastly refused. But Tyrus' passionate response to purple (never before seen, as the story goes) overwhelms her. She weakens and agrees to marry Melkart, provided the betrothal is sealed with the gift of a purple robe.

But there is nothing romantic about how murex is made. Soft mollusc bodies contain a hypobranchial gland full of sticky fluid (a dye precursor) that, when exposed to air, oxidizes from yellow to a brilliant purple. Because the hypobranchial sac is so small and contains so little fluid (a substance the animal uses to stun its prey), both fluid extraction and dyeing with *Murex* (and related species: see p. 13) are tedious operations. Labour was cheap in the ancient world. Nor did the stench matter, for then as now the unpleasant odor was what identified authentic murex. A gram of dye required thousands of shellfish; this depleted the resource and inflated the price. But before molluscs were completely wiped out, someone discovered that lichens produced a purple dye identical to murex. The combination of murex and lichens was thus an economic response to an ecological and environmental crisis—the over-exploitation of a natural resource.

Roman Murex and Orchil

Why was purple so popular in Rome? Conspicuous consumption is the answer. The Romans used purple to proclaim rank. Expensive clothing declared status and wealth. Historians also claim that purple garments worn in battle camouflaged wounds, so the enemy could not see the damage inflicted. But the most compelling reason for wearing purple was snobbery. Roman purple was notorious for another reason: the male and female purple dyers (the famous "Purpurii") died at an unusually young age—little wonder, with tools of lead. Muthesius also claims the children of female purple dyers were expected to assume their mother's trade, thus perpetuating a dangerous occupation with implications in regard to childbearing and women's health. Their purple-stained skin, according to Pliny, "reeked of fish." His pejorative opinion of the Roman infatuation with purple was as strong, apparently, as the stench of murex.

CHART 1: ORCHIL AND MUREX COMBINATIONS

How orchil was used in murex dyeing	Sources*
orchil used to duplicate murex	Papyrus Holmiensis 3rd century A.D.
orchil used to duplicate murex	Plictho 1548 (Rosetti)
orchil used to improve murex dye colours	Bancroft 1814; Lindsay 1856
orchil used as a murex mordant	Born 1937
orchil used as a murex ground colour	Kok 1966
orchil used to improve fastness of murex	Robinson 1971
orchil used to adjust murex colours	Perkins 1986
orchil used to extend murex	Walton Rogers 1989**; Liles 1990

| *See Bibliography for full citations | **See note p. 23 |

Bronze and Iron Age Lichen Dyes

To the early Christians, purple was the colour of sin and self-indulgence. But this value judgement does nothing to explain why the manufacture of orchil continued at Constantinople, the centre of Christianity. This information is in direct contradiction to encyclopedias and other sources that claim orchil "died out" after the fall of Rome. Once we had no more than Kok's assertion that the manufacture of orchil spread during the Dark Ages to European monasteries, where skilled artisans kept the process alive. Now there is actual evidence.

Recent findings show there were several Bronze and Iron Age lichen dyes that were technically not orchil (e.g., *Roccella*, p. 17), but northern, vernacular orchil equivalents. Evidence of Anglo-Norse and Hiberno-Norse dyes from burials in Denmark and Greenland shows that northern lichen species were used. Lab analysis (Taylor; Taylor and Walton Rogers) has provided a library of visual spectra for comparative purposes: these samples prove that northern AM dyes match purples made not from *Roccella*, but from lichens including *Ochrolechia*, *Lasallia* and *Umbilicaria*. Like the purple robe excavated in China, northern lichen-dyed textiles provide convincing archaeological evidence that purple lichen dyes did survive the Dark Ages. This broadens the Bronze and Iron Age record for lichen dyes. It also adds substance to the speculation that other AM lichen dyes may have rivaled orchil in regard to local manufacture and production at specific sites in Britain and continental Europe.

Florentine Orchil

Just when did Federigo return home from the Crusades with the orchil formula? Some say it was as late as the 15th century, but Kok is of the opinion that the Rucellai (p. 5) began their orchil operation as early as the 12th century. A new middle class was emerging, one that had a taste for luxuries, and orchil became popular throughout Europe. The Rucellai saga described by Woodward is one of a very successful "family business." But Perkins claims it was more broadly based in economic terms, an export monopoly that lasted for centuries. She contends that the Rucellai controlled the supply of Mediterranean *Roccella* and set the price. The excessively high cost of orchil may explain why vernacular lichen dyes found a market niche. For example, cork was available in England circa 1100 (Hunt). Furley also provides evidence of a 14th-century French/English cork trade centered at Winchester. As cork (p. 23) is made from *Ochrolechia*, these early citations strongly suggest the need to revise the story of dye history. For example, new interpretations of material culture will likely confirm a northern orchil equivalent manufactured in Ireland—if O'Curry is right—as early as the 9th century. (That the lichen he mentions is *Umbilicaria* is remarkable, for I observed in 1985 that it is locally abundant only in Donegal.)

Medieval and Renaissance Lichen Dyes

Medieval guilds perpetuated a system of strict controls to regulate textile production. The mystery and alchemy involved in dyeing (blood, dung and arsenic were standard additives) fed popular superstitions of the day. Implicit in guild regulations were threats to body and health. Dyers who divulged trade secrets were severely punished: supposedly, the loss of a hand was considered appropriate. Threats of physical harm were likely a deterrent to prevent competition, and so it is not surprising that medieval lichen-dye recipes were vague. A lack of scientific knowledge, and vagueness regarding common names, compounded the problem. Dye lichens were known variously as "herb l'orseille" (confused with herbs), "maw' se" (misconstrued as moss), "rags" (mistaken for ragwort) and "weeds of the sea" (misidentified as seaweed). By comparison, home remedies of the day were straightforward. Popular herbals promoted the Doctrine of Signatures, whereby plants were used to cure the body parts they most resembled. For example, *Lobaria pulmonaria*, which resembles lung tissue, was a cure for congestion. This medicinal profile conflicts with the fact that there are fewer lichen-dye recipes from this period than from the preceding millennium (see Casselman 1999a).

Dye books claim that BWM dyes (see Glossary) have been in use "forever." But this claim is not supported by evidence. To date, I have not found a singlemedieval recipe for BWM dyes (p. 12).Nonexistent recipes are a problem, especially when one discovers there is an abundance of medieval documentation for AM dyes (Casselman 1999a). Ryan and O'Riordan record the earliest BWM recipe I have collected: a 1749 yellow BWM dye from *Haematomma*. Two other 18th-century citations I have found include a 1752 Danish recipe for *Peltigera canina* (Wold and Nielsen). From Ireland, there is also Rutty's 1772 "stone-crottles" in Hill's modern facsimile. So, unlike orchil and cork, BWM dyes appear to be virtually absent in literature from the 13th to 17th centuries. Brown and gold are less valuable colours; is this why there are no recipes? Were they less popular? Or have we not yet looked in all the right places? Although I cannot confirm Grierson's vague mention of a late 17th-century BWM dye, I suspect that more cooperation among researchers and a lexicon of vernacular dye names would help to solve the mystery.

The Industrial Revolution and Lichen Dyes

Lichen dyes played an important role in the Industrial Revolution. Although the British dye industry lagged behind that of Europe, there was political and financial pressure to develop local dyes from indigenous plants. Thus, the discovery of cudbear—a native red dye that was cheaper than imported orchil—was a sign of progress. Today, it is difficult to appreciate the appalling social conditions that were part of the booming textile industry. Remember the Roman Purpurii and those medieval dyers? Try now, if you will, to conjure an image of the cudbear factory circa 1760. It is the time of the Clearances, and although we picture families driven off the land to make room for sheep, not all crofters leave the Highlands. Some that remain are those whose meagre income is based entirely on harvesting dye lichens. But lichens weigh very little; an entire family must work days to gather the equivalent of 100 pounds of lichen, an amount that at the factory is worth only a few pence.

Even city-dwellers in tenement slums are drawn into the cudbear industry. The urban poor not only save urine, but collect it for landlords who sell "graith" to the dye factories. Worse off than the urine collectors are those workers who spend their days filtering hundreds of gallons of urine, for fecal contamination spoils the dye. (Read Bancroft's description of tests using two types of cudbear—one made with urine containing feces and one without "the offensive addition"—for what may be the most odoriferous account of dye experimentation in all of textile history!)

Compared to this, it is an easy job to pick out debris. But the shredding machines have menacing mangles. Crystals of quartzite cling to the lichens and foul the gears; when production time is lost, workers are docked pay. In another part of the factory, huge paddles mix a paste of lichens and urine before the cudbear is poured into troughs to ferment. The addition of water and sloshing of the mash help to incorporate oxygen in the lichen sludge, for aeration is essential to the development of orcein. After 3 weeks, a sample of the concentrated dye is poured onto a slab of marble, where a dramatic blackish-purple stain on the white stone indicates the cudbear is ready to use. Now the dye is treated one of several ways: either it is diluted with water and used immediately; or it is dehydrated, dried to a powder, then mixed with lime or chalk and formed into cakes. Cudbear is popular because of the low price, a bargain when compared with Mediterranean orchil, made from imported *Roccella*, and the equally expensive and exotic imports cochineal and kermes.

But in the end, it is the legendary beauty of this red Scottish lichen dye that makes cudbear famous as both a domestic product and an export item. And cudbear might well have rivaled orchil in longevity had not the legacy been cut short. A number of problems arose. Carelessness in gathering the lichens (e.g., harvesting the "wrong kind": p. 13), and on-going financial problems (below) led to a decline in quality and increase in manufacturing inconsistencies. Were the new aniline dyes, developed by 1860, the reason why the first indigenous red dye produced on an industrial scale within the British Isles was shoved aside? Was it the more somber Victorian palette? Or is there another story here, one that remains untold? (See Epilogue).

The Cudbear Industry

Cudbear was developed in Scotland by the Gordon family. Patented in 1758, the dye was named for Mrs. Gordon (née Cuthbert) and a son who helped turn his mother's domestic dye into an entire industry. The family saga begins in the 1750s in Foddaletter, a Highland village in Banffshire. Cuthbert and George Gordon, and their partner, William Alexander, opened the first cudbear factory in Leith, a district of Edinburgh. According to Clow and Clow, there were other partnerships formed and dissolved over the years. Eventually, there was a huge cudbear factory in Glasgow from which emanated the colourful folklore that Scottish historians associate with these barons of industry and the dye that made their fortunes rise and fall.

As with other boom-and-bust cycles, the cudbear market developed quickly, then sharply declined. For 30 years, the Gordons struggled to promote their northern lichen dye, which was, in their opinion, just as good a dye as imported orchil. True, cudbear was cheaper to make, for

Ochrolechia tartarea was then common in the Highlands. But just as *Roccella* crept into murex, imported Norwegian lichens (*Lasallia* and *Umbilicaria*) were used in cudbear when Scottish *Ochrolechia* ran out. Apparently unknown to the Gordons was the fact that the lichens used to supplement *Ochrolechia* required a longer processing time (see Chart 2a, p. 17). Is this detail what made the difference to the Lunds in Norway?

Stories about cudbear involve intrigue. At the outset, there was the problem of industrial espionage. The Gordon family brought a novel approach to human resources: they not only hired Gaelic-speaking workers (who would less likely mingle with English-speaking outsiders), but also kept them at work and rest inside high factory walls. And what walls—according to Clow and Clow, one cudbear factory covered 17 acres! But in the long run, the cudbear process (which was essentially no different from that of korkje, p. 12) escaped. According to Llano, by 1800 it was impossible to tell the difference between English orchil and Scottish cudbear: as with murex and orchil, biological necessity dictated that the two products merge. The Gordons promoted their product as a local initiative to help boost the rural economy. But the cudbear industry, like other industrial processes in a boom-and-bust economic cycle, ravaged the native lichen flora of Highland Scotland and the north of England. When the demand for cudbear was high, harvesters gathered any lichen they could find, and this perception of prodigality gave rise to the notion that crottle is *any lichen whatsoever*. According to Lindsay, the eventual depletion of Highland lichens led to the importation of umbilicate species from Norway and Sweden.

As bankruptcy loomed, the Gordons appealed for funding. They lobbied the government to ban imported red dyes. But nothing could avoid the financial mayhem that ensued when the industry failed. The reasons were economic, ecological and aesthetic. The public began to acquire different tastes, influenced by the removal of trade barriers that resulted in an influx of continental fabrics. And it was just as well, for dye lichens were over-harvested to such an extent that once-common species were, by the early 1800s, in serious decline. A similar situation occurred in France (Dallon).

Norwegian Korkje

The Norwegian lichen-dye industry is less well known. This is puzzling. The Lunds of Farsund, on the Lista peninsula of southwest Norway, manufactured a red dye based on *Ochrolechia*, a dye identical to Scottish cudbear. Does the comparison extend further? For example, when *Ochrolechia* became scarce in Norway, were umbilicate lichens used as well? Is the answer to be found today, 250 years later, in the lichen diversity and abundance of southwest Norway? That question led me in 1992 to Lista, where there is little *O. tartarea* today, but, paradoxically, a bountiful supply of umbilicate species. Did what happened to cudbear (the over-harvesting of *Ochrolechia*) happen also to korkje? Or is the Norwegian story different?

Archaeological evidence of early Norse lichen dyes (p. 7) proves that northern AM dyes such as korkje are an ancient tradition. Korkje, like cudbear, created a rural economic boom. Korkje profits enabled the Lunds to build the largest wooden house in Norway. Today, this imposing building serves as the Farsund town hall (photo: Casselman 1993e). Nor is the mystery of korkje success lessened when one learns, as I did from Samuel Watnee, that the Lunds sent a son to Scotland to confer with the Gordons. To whose benefit? Was a joint business venture planned, possibly a merger? It is interesting to speculate. What explains why korkje, a financial success, is overshadowed in textile history by cudbear, an *identical* dye that failed? That a Scottish dye also included Norwegian lichens is as inexplicable as korkje's apparent success.

Why did some commercial lichen-dye operations end in failure? Was it because the chemistry of lichen substances was not fully understood? Llano feels this was likely the case. For unless one understands how to exploit lichen pigments effectively, and the methodological difference in regard to AM dyes (depending upon which species are used: Chart 2a, p. 17), the process remains as mysterious as alchemy. But fame is alluring, and the idea that humble organisms can create wealth and enshrine a family in history may explain why the Rucellai, the Gordons, and the Lunds were smitten by the charisma of lichen dyes—as I have been myself for almost 30 years.

CHAPTER NOTES (see also Glossary)

AM, BWM dyes AM (ammonia method) dyes involve a chemical process of putrefaction in which lichen particles, urine and water are fermented (aged in a vat) for 3–16 weeks or more to develop orcein (Chart 3b, p. 28). The urine has been replaced by ammonia in the modern AM process, hence the name "ammonia method" dyes (coined by Brough as "AFM"). BWM (boiling water method) dyes involve a direct dye process in which lichen acids are extracted in boiling water (Chart 3a, p. 26).

Murex Murex recipes are notoriously vague in regard to the actual method (Edmonds is a notable exception). Some say the entire mollusc is first crushed to remove the hypobranchial gland. Others claim the gland is removed intact, leaving the animal alive. The next step is to combine the fluid (drained or squeezed from the hypobranchial sac) with salt and water. The mixture is apparently ready for use within several days. Gerhard describes "milking" large Central American molluscs; what he means is that a sharp probe is inserted into the mollusc that forces it to eject the fluid. For my own experiments, I extract the hypobranchial gland first, prick the sac with a sharp instrument, then smear the fluid directly onto fabric (a tedious and odoriferous process). Asian species used include *Murex* and *Purpura;* for experiments at the Humboldt Institute, Steuben, Maine (1998–2000), we used *Thais lapillus.* And we were able to verify that the labour involved and unevenness in application are the primary limitations of mollusc dyes.

Orchil Pronounced *OR kill*, this AM dye is made the same way as cudbear and korkje: lichen particles, urine (or ammonia) and water are fermented in a vat for 3 weeks (Chart 2a, p. 17). The orchil recipes in the 3rd-century *Papyrus Holmiensis* (p. 7) are actually fraudulent lichen-based purples intended to imitate the more expensive murex. Perhaps because 1,000 years passed before the next lichen dye recipe was published, historians wrongly concluded that orchil "died out" in Europe (p. 7). Arsenic and lead are essential ingredients in the orchil recipe contained in Rosetti's 1548 *Plictho de l'arte de Tentori* (Chart 1, p. 7), illustrated in Casselman 1994b).

Orchil and murex combine Orchil was a ground colour on textiles subsequently over-dyed with murex. This "double dipping" described in the Bible (see Kok) added luster and sheen to silk and helped extend the more expensive dye. Combining dyes made economic and ecological sense, for murex was labour-intensive, increasingly scarce, and inconsistent. Murex application (see above) is notoriously uneven. In contrast, orchil is easy to apply, and it also conveniently hides flaws. (Gardner contains a rhapsodic account of orchil's merits in this regard.)

Cudbear The popularity of cudbear led to a shortage of lichens. When *Ochrolechia* became scarce, *Lasallia* and *Umbilicaria* were added (p. 11). But umbilicate lichens contain different dye acids (Chart 5a, p. 48). Instead of 3 weeks, dyes that contain *Lasallia* and *Umbilicaria* must ferment for at least 16 weeks (Chart 3b, p. 27). Cudbear quality suffered because this essential difference was overlooked or ignored. This fundamental misunderstanding as to the timing of AM vat dyes continues today. The so-called "orchil" pictured in Van Stralen is not *Roccella*, but *Umbilicaria;* and the method described (i.e. aging for several days an AM vat that requires many weeks) is inadequate for the development of orcein.

Korkje Pronounced *CORE sha*, this Norse dye has an ancient past supported by archaeological evidence of a Bronze and/or Iron Age provenance. Several similar northern dyes are also recorded (Walton Rogers, p. 23); see also Pritchard, Taylor, and Taylor and Walton Rogers in the Bibliography).

A colour note Throughout textile history, the colour names *red* and *purple* have been used to describe shades from blackish-purple and dark maroon to light pink and bright fuchsia. Although cudbear is described as a "red" lichen dye, and orchil as "purple," there is little difference in the wide range of colours produced by AM dyes such as cudbear, korkje, cork, orchil and orsallia.

2

Domestic Lichen Dyes of Northern Europe and North America

Traditional Lichen Dye Methods

A sooty, bubbling cauldron of lichen and fleece hangs over a peat fire: this is the popular image of traditional "crottle" dyeing, a portrayal reinforced by movies and travel writers. There lingers a perception that the Scottish Highlands and islands are the only places where lichen dyes are made, a misconception that fuels textile tourism. Ironically, individual craft praxis has increased in North America just as cottage industry crottle dyeing has declined in the Outer Hebrides. The irony extends to lichen dye research, now centered well beyond the British Isles. But it is true that lichen dyes represent 2,000 years of an unbroken Anglo, Celtic, and Norse tradition (Casselman 1994a–1999b).

Traditional methods are generally vague and technical adaptations many. For example, "contact" dyeing was widely practiced in Scotland and Ireland, but an exhaustive survey of BWM recipes shows no two BWM methods are exactly the same. "Take two creels of crotal, and lay in fleece and add more crotal 'til the kettle is full up," begins one 19th-century Aran method in typical fashion. You *do* begin by layering lichens and wool in an iron pot. But some books advise to pre-soak the lichens in water or they suggest soaking the lichens and wool together. An iron cauldron and rain water are reported to give the best results (Richardson 1975). After the lichens, wool and water are combined in the dye pot, the mixture is heated. Characteristic of recipe variation, some say to boil the BWM dye bath for 1 hour; other recipes suggest several days or even a week (p. 17). The dyer then removes the pot from the heat, cools it

15

overnight and repeats this sequence one or more times, until the yarn reaches the desired colour. (You "peek" into the layers of lichen and fibre to check the colour.) While technical methodology is hardly the term for this instinctive and intuitive approach, it does work. And travel writers love it (see also Epilogue).

Most AM recipes begin with a description of how to collect the lichens. There is no agreement as to the "right" time for *Ochrolechia*: spring, summer and fall are all suggested. Once you have gathered the appropriate species (and where to find them is, according to most sources, "a family secret"), the lichens are crumbled and mixed with ammonia and water to form a thick slurry. Some "set" (age) the vat for a mere few weeks, but modern dyers are advised differently: see Chart 2a.

And when is the AM vat ready? Imagine a dyer today who would be willing to *taste* a dye vat, but according to Westring, that was one way to tell in 1805. A safer method is to be guided by the timing (Chart 3b, p. 27). Preparation of the AM dye bath is easy, yet instructions (p. 26) are generally missing from older recipes. Was it common knowledge or were there economic advantages to be gained by keeping the process a secret?

Domestic Scottish Lichen Dyes

Strictly speaking, "crottle" is the correct term not for dyes, but for two specific lichens, *Parmelia omphalodes* and *Parmelia saxatilis* (Casselman 1994b). Some say "crotal" is the Irish Gaelic spelling, but even on this technicality, there is little agreement. In the past, "crottle" or "crotal" was used to describe not only the dyes themselves, but any and all dye lichens, which led to much confusion. Each dyer made her own version of crottle. Unrecorded recipes were passed along as "secrets" within circles of kinship. According to historical accounts, dyeing was a seasonal ritual: women and children gathered the lichens while older women prepared the fleece. Fraser's verbatim recipe for Skye *crotal dubh* (dark crottle) goes as follows: "Put ply about [sic] crottle and wool in cold water, bring to a boil and simmer for two hours. Pour off the water and dry the material." Fraser gives a Loch Boisdale recipe that involves heating the crottle, wool and water for 6 hours, then "standing the dye for a day" before removing the dyed wool. Both produce a shade of orange or rusty brown.

Grierson 1986 gives ecological details that enrich a traditional Uist recipe: ". . . in one district all of the women collected their crotal—the dark kind, [*Parmelia omphalodes*], from one particular hill" because "as far back as anyone could remember" the lichens from that hill produced "the brightest colours." (Note that Grierson's Hebridean spelling is "crotal," as in Ireland.) She continues: ". . . the gatherers were careful not to return to the same rocks for a number of years" (*ibid.*).

CHART 2a: COMMON LICHEN DYE NAMES AND INGREDIENTS

Dye name & type	Lichen used	Time required	Colours*
orchil AM	*Roccella* spp.	3 weeks	red/purple
crottle/crotal BWM	*Parmelia omphalodes* and/or *P. saxatilis*	3–5 days	rust/copper/ orange/brown
cudbear[#] AM	*Ochrolechia tartarea*; later *Lasallia* and/or *Umbilicaria* spp.[†]	6–8 weeks Chart 3b, p. 20)	red/purple
orsallia[§] AM	*Actinogyra, Lasallia & Umbilicaria*	16 weeks (Chart 3b)	red/purple red/purple

*Achieved without mordants or pH adjustment.
[#]Other vernacular AM dyes include "cork" & "korkje."
[†]Eventually umbilicate lichens were substituted: see p. 7.
[§]These species are combined; see p. 27.

No reference to Scottish lichen dyes is complete without mention of Harris tweed. Everyone who has worn this indestructible cloth recalls the aroma of the wool. (A discussion of this point enlivened the editing process of the Sharnoff lichen article in *National Geographic*. Editors pressured me to use the word "musty" to describe crottle-dyed wool, but as their "expert," I held out for the less pejorative "earthy.") Originally, Harris tweed featured all-natural dyes. But long after lichens ceased to be used, Harris tweed promotional materials claimed that crottle gave Harris tweed cloth its distinctive aroma and colour.

Except for special fabrics presented to dignitaries, lichen dyes were rarely used after World War II, despite the folklore. One way to tell is to sniff the fabric, for crottle imparts an aroma that a practiced nose can detect. The extent to which travel writers portray lichen dyeing as a routine seasonal activity, especially on the Hebrides, is apparent in articles such as Yeadon. This portrayal is a misrepresentation that construes the display of lichens in the dyer's studio as evidence of current practice. Does this matter? Not when the activity is accurately described as "re-enactment." (What of the popular milling frolics held for tourists in Scotland and in Cape Breton?) But we risk what Greenhalgh calls "false tradition" if we transform domestic textile labour—including lichen dyeing—into romance.

Irish Lichen Dyes

Just as Scottish lichen dyes are linked to Harris tweed, dyes made from Irish "crotal" are integral to the story of Donegal tweed. Hoad's account is rich in detail. For example, weft yarns were crotal-dyed before spinning. (Imagine the crotal-dyed weft required for an 80-pound warp!) Tweed dyeing was done over an outdoor turf fire and involved huge pots. How much dyestuff was actually used? While equal amounts of lichen and fibre (by weight) applied to plant dyes in general, Hoad claims this was not the case for crotal. One used "just as much as you need to get a good colour," or the equivalent of a 1:2 ratio (half as much lichen as fibre). Scottish ratios are typically 2:1 (twice as much lichen as fibre, according to Lindsay). In rural Sweden, Llano documented a 4:1 BWM ratio (4 times as much lichen as fibre). These wasteful formulas in northern Europe were the result of a perceived prodigality that later provided ammunition for the anti-dye lobby in the 1970s.

Irish crotal methods seem to involve longer cooking than do Scottish recipes based on *Parmelia omphalodes* and *P. saxatilis*. Hoad gives two methods: one is an adaptation of the contact method, in which lichens are cooked alone for 1 or 2 days, then "reboiled with the wool." The other is the standard contact method, in which lichens are processed for "as long as a week." Cork (p. 23) based on *Ochrolechia*—supposedly gathered in May and June—was stirred "6 times a day for 15 to 28 days," according to Mitchell. (Compare with Chart 3b, p. 27.) While colourful to read, the dyer today must reinterpret such recipes within a broader context that more clearly defines AM and BWM methodologies and nuances such as temperature (p. 27).

The lichens used for dyes are very similar in Ireland, the Outer Hebrides, Wales, northern England, Highland and island Scotland, and Scandinavia. And yet historians claim that red and purple AM dyes were more popular with the Scots than with the Irish and the Norse. Such claims are erroneous. (Can we blame them on the accumulation of confusing dye names?) In *Textiles From Coppergate*, Walton Rogers describes purple as "the most prevalent colour in Viking Dublin." Archaeological evidence confirms literature reports that Irish AM dyes are as ancient a technology as Mediterranean orchil. Furthermore, Irish records in O'Curry now predate the earliest Scottish AM dyes. Is this Hiberno-Norse tradition a clue that northern AM dyes may have originated in Viking-dominated regions and spread from there to Britain, *rather than the reverse*? The presumption of Scottish origins for all AM lichen dyes in the North Atlantic region must now be challenged.

Immigrant Irish and Scottish lichen-dye recipes in eastern North America are the subject of my ongoing research; in the meantime, there are two fascinating references to lichens in 19th-century Ontario. One is Susannah Moodie's famous description of the man whose ecstasy is inspired by lichens, also quoted in Richardson 1975. And in *Away*, the dispirited Irish immigrant portrayed by novelist Jane Urquhart uses *Lobaria pulmonaria* as a substitute for yeast.

Scandinavian Lichen Dyes

Scandinavian lichen dyes are much older than previously thought. For example, there is archaeological evidence of Iron Age Norse AM dyes. There is also a considerable record for the medieval period (Høiland), and 13th-century Greenland "purples" of exceptional quality are described by Walton Rogers (1993). Linnaeus mentions 18th-century lichen dyes, but Westring remains the most reliable Scandinavian source. Yet Westring is conspicuous by his absence in most 20th-century dye books written in Denmark, Finland, Norway, Sweden, Iceland, and the Færoe Islands. (Another valuable source of 18th-century European lichen dyes is Hoffmann 1787.) Thanks to George Llano and my husband, Ted, I now own a copy of Westring 1805. A valuable research exercise would be a comparison of Westring and Hoffmann. But my attempts to see Hoffmann's book failed after arrangements with the British Library (made weeks in advance and confirmed on paper) fell through. After flying to London and waiting at the library for 3 days, I was told by the staff that the book was "at the bindery." Llano (who recalls seeing it many years ago) verifies that Hoffmann's 1787 (whether "at the bindery" or missing) is outstanding (see Epilogue).

Important sources like Hoffmann, Westring and Lindsay are useful to modern dyers because they provide a link between traditional and modern methods. In Sweden, textile historian Gösta Sandberg and his colleague, chemist Jan Sisefsky, have adapted traditional lichen dyes for modern artisans. At Nora, Sandberg's library contains hundreds of dye books that span four centuries, including two copies of Westring. Sisefsky has also studied the biochemistry of lichen dyes, and this work is now available in a 1997 English edition of Sandberg's book on red dyes.

Many Norwegian writers mention korkje in an unfavorable light (Casselman 1999b). I attribute this to a profound misunderstanding of AM methodology and, in Dagmar Lunde's case, possible use of the wrong lichens. This negative legacy is why, according to what the authors told me, AM dyes are not included in Lye and Lye (see Chart 3d, p. 34).

Early American Lichen Dyes

The first records of lichen dye use in North America that I have found concern an AM dye from Pennsylvania (Kalm: see Benson 1966) and a

Labrador BWM dye (Isham). The "red" Pennsylvania dye may represent the first documented lichen dye use in Colonial America, while Isham's "maw'se" is arguably the *first aboriginal use* of lichens as pigments recorded anywhere in North America. (For the significance of these dyes in sociocultural terms, see Diadick Casselman 1999a.)

Adrosko has produced an impressive tally of 18th- and 19th-century dye manuals; yet she admits that "scanty information means we will never know the full extent of home dyeing in colonial America." Instructional manuals noted by Adrosko fall into two categories: those that originated elsewhere (notably in England, France or Germany: Bancroft is one example) and those few that were published in America (e.g., Bemiss). Adrosko points out the fine distinction: some American authors adapted European recipes when they came to America, then added material for local consumption. Up to about 1850, however, Adrosko claims most professional dyers in America were trained in Europe. Is this Eurocentric influence the reason why lichen dye "firsts" in North America involve primarily European observers like Isham and Kalm, who note typical European lichens?

Dyestuffs involved enormous profits. Botanists were sent to North America as "economic spies" to seek out valuable plants for export to Europe. A student of Linnaeus, Pehr Kalm was one of these. The Pennsylvania lichen is described by Kalm as *Hoffmann's muscorum*, named for the lichenologist G. F. Hoffmann. "Muscorum" describes a warty, greyish-white, crustose lichen that suggests *Ochrolechia tartarea*. To so identify *Hoffmann's muscorum* would solve the mystery, except for a fact of geography. One expert (Dr. I. Brodo) considers this species to be rare south of the Great Lakes. Another authority (Dr. D.H.S. Richardson) suggests "muscorum" might be *Diploschistes* (see Chart 3c, p. 31), a lichen that does occur in Pennsylvania. Furthermore, to add to the confusion, Ure links to Kalm a reference to *Umbilicaria*, a genus that bears no resemblance whatsoever to either *Diploschistes* or *Ochrolechia*! So there are at least three explanations for Kalm's dye. Compared to the problems associated with identifying the lichen involved, it is fairly easy to categorize the Pennsylvania dye as to type (because of the result: red) and mode of production (apparently urine was used).

From early American botanists, we know that many suitable dye lichens were available in eastern North America (Casselman 1994b). Is this prodigality the reason why there lingers a perception that lichen dyeing was widely practiced in 18th- and 19th-century Appalachia? In a region where traditional crafts thrive, the virtual absence of lichen dyeing, in contrast to the perception, presents a disparity that is not easily explained. Fred Gerber claims that Appalachian lichen dyes are a "depauperate remnant" of a settler tradition that, for some reason, failed to flourish. In Gerber's opinion, there is a "missing link" between European and American lichen dye traditions (pers. comm., Oak Ridge, Tenn., Nov. 4, 1993). There is evidence to support this view: lichen dyes are conspicuous by their absence in Emma Conley's *Vegetable Dyeing;* Mary Frances Davidson's *The Dye-Pot;* and Frances Louisa Goodrich's *Mountain Homespun.* The single exception in Appalachian manuals appears to be the BWM dyes in Furry and Viemont.

Lichen dyeing may have remained a more viable skill in Canada in areas such as rural Quebec, Prince Edward Island, and Cape Breton Island (Nova Scotia). Here there is evidence that a flourishing French culture, along with the influence of Gaelic settlers, perpetuated a "need and necessity" model, evidenced in archival sources (Diadick Casselman 1999a).

American Aboriginal Lichen Dyes

James Isham was a Hudson's Bay factor whose journal (circa 1750) depicts northern life. Orcadians and Shetlanders were numerous among the company's employees. Well-educated for the times, they brought with them to northern Canada floras of their home islands. And in these floras of the period, lichens were routinely referred to as "maw'se." Isham describes a lichen dye that is noteworthy on three counts: the intensity and beauty of the yellow dye; the ease of preparation (Isham claims the "maw'se" or lichen is simply "boilt in hot water"); and the number of porcupine quills dyed with just a "handful" of lichens. These indicators point to a BWM lichen such as *Cetraria* or *Letharia*, both of which produce strong yellows.

A paper on modern Navajo AM and BWM methods (Brough 1988) is the best source for North American information on aboriginal lichen dyes, which are curiously omitted from Densmore's Chippewa study and appear to have been mostly overlooked by Leechman, a much-quoted Canadian ethnologist. Bearfoot includes a recipe with the accompanying folklore that lichen dyes are more fast if the yarn is dried on rocks. Goward—a lichenologist, like Brough—mentions aboriginal clothing made from lichens. Turner, an ethnobotanist, includes in one of her articles a photograph of a remarkable pair of shoes made from lichens. Additional human uses of lichens for hygiene, healing and ritual, are discussed in *The Gorsebrook Papers* (Diadick Casselman 2001).

CHART 2b: SOME TRADITIONAL LICHEN DYES
FROM 23 COUNTRIES

Country	Sources*	Lichens used	Dye type
Australia	Gordon	*Pseudocyphellaria crocata*	AM, BWM
Canada (First Peoples)	Turner	*Alectoria fremontii*	BWM
Canada (French)	Bériau	many species	AM, BWM
Denmark	Wold and Nielsen	*Peltigera canina*	BWM
Denmark (Færoe Islands)	Bærentsen	*Ochrolechia tartarea*	AM
England	See pp. 31–36	many species	AM, BWM
Finland	Konturri	several species	AM, BWM
France	Dallon	*Ochrolechia parella*	AM
Germany	Hoffmann, G. F.	many species	AM, BWM
Iceland	Swenson (Weigle 1973)	*Cetraria islandica*	AM
India	Seshadri	*Roccella* species	AM
Indonesia	Hofmann, R.	*Ramalina* species	as mordant
Ireland	Rutty (Hill 1990)	several species	AM, BWM
Italy	Rosetti	*Roccella* species	AM
Japan	Teramura	several species	AM, BWM
Mexico	Perkins	*Roccella* species	AM
New Zealand	Milner	several species	AM, BWM
Norway	Høiland	*Ochrolechia*	AM
Norway	Lye and Lye	many species	BWM
Peru	Antúnez de Mayolo	several species	BWM
Portugal	Perkins	*Roccella* species	AM
Scotland	Lindsay 1856	many species	AM, BWM
Sweden	Sandberg and Sisefsky	many species	AM, BWM
Switzerland	Lindsay 1854	many species	AM, BWM
USA	Kalm	See pp. 31–36	AM
USA(First Peoples)	Brough	many species	AM, BWM

Note: *See Bibliography for full citations; see also Charts 3c and 3d
      "Several" = fewer than 4 or 5 species

CHAPTER NOTES

Dye names There is still no critical study on the etymology of vernacular names for lichen dyes (see Epilogue); names are applied inconsistently. A sampling includes archel, archil and arcel (English); byttelet (Swedish); crotal (Irish, Scottish, Hebridean); crottle (English, Scottish); fucus (Latin); cork, corker and korc (English, Irish, Scottish); corcur, corkir, korkir and korkalit (Gaelic); kenkering (Welsh); korki (Færoese); korkje (Norwegian); lacunus (Dutch); lak (Norwegian); orcella (Italian); orchella and orchilla (Spanish); oricella (Arabic); oricello (German, Italian); orn-

massa (Swedish); orseille (French); orseille de l'herbe (French); parelle (French); persio and persis (Spanish); phukh (Hebrew); phukos (Greek); tusch lav (Swedish); and urzella (Portuguese). Compare orsallia, Chart 2a, p. 17.

Cork Some writers claim that "cork" is just another name for cudbear. "Corc," "cork" and "korc" are erroneously used as references to *any and all* AM dyes, including cudbear, orchil and korkje. To add to the confusion, some writers use "cork" to describe even BWM dyes. Strictly speaking, "dark crottle" and "light crottle" describe not the dyes, but the lichens used to make BWM dyes. And when correctly applied, "crottle" refers specifically to only two lichens: *Parmelia omphalodes* and *P. saxatilis* (p. 16; Casselman 1994b). To avoid future problems, "cork" should also be applied exclusively to AM dyes made primarily with *Ochrolechia tartarea*, a usage that reflects the historical record (see Furley; also Hunt).

Archaeology and Norse dyes Walton Rogers uses absorption spectrometry as a scanning procedure, and TLC (see Glossary) to detect lichen pigments on excavated textiles (p. 7). Along with various colleagues Textile Research Associates have singly and collectively done studies that illuminate the growing body of evidence in support of Bronze and Iron Age lichen pigments, dyes that parallel Mediterranean/Asian orchil. These studies have advanced textile historiography and a rewriting of the story of dyes will show how and why this has happened. (Bibliographic note: *Dyes in History and Archaeology* is both an annual academic meeting where papers are presented and the title of the annual proceedings published by various institutions; see Cooksey, Dallon and Hofmann.) The DHA title has also undergone changes over the years (compare Taylor and Walton 1983 and Walton 1989a). The acronym "DHAT" now refers to the yearly meeting, and to the collected papers that comprise the proceedings.

Traditional recipes Bolton, Edmondston, Fraser, Goodwin, Grierson, Kok, Lindsay, Llano, Maclagan, Richardson, Robertson, Simmons, Thurston, and many others describe old Scottish lichen dyes. Kok and Llano focus on the economic aspect of cudbear; see Llano 1951 for Harris tweed information. Bolton, Goodwin, Robertson and Wickens are enjoyable, but Grierson, Kok, Llano, Maclagan and Richardson 1975 add historical veracity. See Edmondston and Fraser for dye folklore, and Høiland and Kok for medieval Norse references. Mitchell and Rutty describe old Irish dyes. Lindsay 1854 and Solberg contain lengthy charts of dye results with a focus on lichen substances. Llano 1944 includes a bibliography of more than 100 little-known European sources.

Lindsay William Lauder Lindsay was a 19th-century Perth physician and dye enthusiast. Administrator of an insane asylum, Lindsay reduced stress by pursuing a passion for lichens. In a series of papers and one book, he described dozens of traditional Gaelic lichen dyes. Lindsay also tried to promote lichen dyeing as a means to economic salvation in rural Scotland. (This initiative, and similar Hebridean projects, are discussed in *The Gorsebrook Papers*.) Published in 1856, Lindsay's *Popular History of British Lichens* is still available at many university libraries. Grierson 1989 includes an illustration of Lindsay's dye samples. (That this "sample book" has since gone missing from Leeds University [see Epilogue] is a great loss to scholarship.) Interestingly, at one point Lindsay was invited to work for the Canadian government. He came for a visit, said "yes" to the offer, later changed his mind, and died shortly after returning to Scotland.

Westring A medical doctor and lichenologist, Johan Pehr Westring was physician to the Royal Court of Sweden. His other responsibility was to teach botany to the court. Westring wrote some French lichen dye articles (published in 1792–94), followed by a series of pamphlets on lichen dyes. Written between 1805 and 1809, these Swedish pamphlets—bound—comprise Westring's "book." Unlike Lindsay, Westring did not self-illustrate; the superb renderings of lichens in what is now known as "Westring 1805" were done by Acharius, a leading lichenologist of the time. Westring believed, as Lindsay did, that lichen dyeing could provide economic benefits in remote areas. *The Maine Naturalist* (Casselman 1994b) includes on the cover an illustration from Westring 1805 and my own dye samples from Swedish *Lasallia pustulata*.

Lichens as cosmetics, cures and treatments Scandinavian lichen-based treatments were popular into this century: Llano's "Economic Uses of Lichens" includes some lichen cures, complete with testimonials. Lichens are still widely used in the cosmetic industry to make perfumes, henna, and shampoo. And informants worldwide have described to me lichens in the marketplaces of Saudi Arabia, India, and Japan, where their uses are primarily culinary. A well-known Maine company produces an underarm deodorant based on lichens. Moxham questions the ethics of harvesting lichens for perfumes when the workers live in poverty. The lichen wreaths currently featured by Martha Stewart also give the unfortunate impression that lichens are "free for the taking."

3

Safe Lichen Dye Methods and Techniques

Safe Lichen Dyes

Salvage botany is nonexploitive collecting of organic material that will otherwise be wasted. Lichens already detached from substrate—those that blow down during winter storms, for example—are ideal for dyeing. Also suitable are urban lichens removed from cemeteries or roofs; lichens on firewood; and lichens collected at sites where human activity puts them at risk (e.g., road construction). A church in my community sheds bagfuls of lichen that are blown off the roof each winter, and the lawn nearby yields even more.

Lichens contain substances (acids: p. 48) that are dye precursors. So theoretically, all lichens can be used for dyes. But there is a geographical and chemical variation in lichen substances; some are better than others. To avoid waste and disappointment, use only the most abundant lichens or those species known to give reliable dyes. Charts 3c and 3d (pp. 31–36) list more than 100 common species used worldwide.

BWM Lichen Dyes

Make your first dye bath a "test" using a few lichens removed from a fallen branch. Remember, you can mix species such as *Hypogymnia physodes* and *Parmelia sulcata*. Approximately 500 ml (2 c) will suffice: see p. 42. Shred the lichens, cover them with water in a dye pot and soak 24–36 hours. Now proceed either way: 1. Put 28 g (1 oz) fibre in with the lichens (the contact method: p. 15); or 2. Cook the lichens first, then add the fibre to the saved liquid. A third alternative is my "triple extraction" method: heat lichens and water to a boil (100°C, 212°F). Maintain the temperature 30 minutes, reduce to simmer (88°C, 190°F) and process 1 hour. Strain off the liquid ("dye liquor") and save it in a clean dye pot or a bucket. Cover lichens with cold water again. Heat, strain off and save the liquor a second time. Then repeat a third time. This accumulated liquor is the dye bath; add the prepared fibre (p. 28). Heat just below a simmer 2–4 hours; leave the fibre in the bath overnight to improve fastness. In my experience, it also helps to add salt (125 ml or ½ c: p. 43) and delay rinsing the fibre (p. 30).

CHART 3a: HOW TO MAKE AM, BWM, AND POD DYES

Type	Colours	Species	How to proceed
AM	red, purple	Chart 3b, 3C	prepare vat (below); dilute vat with water to make dye bath (p. 27)
BWM	gold, rust	Chart 3d	pre-cook lichens in water (p. 15, above); add fibre *or* process lichens and fibre simultaneously
POD	blue	Chart 3c	proceed as AM dye; then expose dyed fibre to sunlight (p. 46); re-dip in dye to intensify effect

AM Lichen Dyes (Orsallia)

There are two types of AM dyes: 1. North American dyes made from umbilicate lichens (e.g., orsallia); and 2. European dyes made from non-umbilicate lichens (Chart 3b). AM dyes require more planning because first you must prepare the vat. To do this, select a glass jar with a snug lid, one that will hold twice the volume of lichen you plan to use: for 250 ml (1 c) of lichen (torn into dime-sized pieces), use a 750-ml (2½ c) jar. (Aeration requires space, and lichens expand considerably as they absorb the liquid you add in the next step.) Start with 250 ml of lichens (it's enough; see * below); combine 125 ml (½ c) water and 125 ml (½ c) household ammonia (1:1 ratio, or see alternative, p. 37). Pour this mixture over the lichens, adding until the lichens are saturated and completely covered. The next step is vat aeration, to incorporate oxygen. Do this by stirring the lichen mixture vigorously, or until large bubbles form. Oxygen is essential in the AM vat. Without it, orcein (see Glossary) will not develop. Once aerated, it is a simple matter to redistribute the oxygen in the vat by

---

*I developed orsallia to encourage ethical lichen-to-fibre ratios. It is a dye formula based on a ratio of 1 part lichen to 10 (or more) parts fibre (by weight). In other words, the amount of lichen used will dye 10 times its weight in fibre. You can also use a mixture of any C+ species (for C test, see p. 48). Appropriate species are in Chart 3c, p. 31).

shaking, instead of actually stirring the contents. Some ignore this step. But in my experience, orcein will not develop fully without proper aeration.

At first, the vat contents will appear brownish-red: this is normal. But as orcinol is converted to orcein, the colour will shift to a dark, saturated magenta. This chemical conversion takes 16 or more weeks with orsallia (Chart 3b, below). Aeration is important: shake the vat 5 or 6 times a day for the first week; 3 times a day for the second week; and once every few days for the remaining 14 weeks. (If the vat remains brownish, see "Troubleshooting," p. 30.)

The actual dye bath is easy to prepare. If your vat contains 500 ml (2 c) of dye liquor, pour off 250 ml (1 c) and dilute this with 4 l (4 qt) of water. Select 1 oz prepared fibre (p. 28) and proceed with the dyeing. If you want a more intense colour, use less fibre or more dye liquor. (Most novice dyers make the mistake of cramming the dye pot, which is how you obtain pastels: see p. 41). Add 125 ml (½ c) salt to the dye bath and heat to a maximum of 82°C (180°F). *Do not boil.* Maintain temperature for 10 minutes; reduce to below 70°C (160°F) and continue to heat gently for 1 hour. Remove pot from the stove and cool overnight. Reheat dye bath the next day to 70°C (160°F) and again cool overnight. Remove fibre; use the delayed rinse (p. 30) and your dye results will improve.

CHART 3b: AM DYES, LICHEN SPECIES USED, AND VAT TIMING

Origin	Name	Lichens used	Substances (acids)	Vat timing
North America	orsallia	*Actinogyra, Lasallia* and *Umbilicaria* species	gyrophoric	minimum 16 weeks
Northern Europe	cork, cudbear, korkje	*Ochrolechia tartarea**	lecanoric**	6–8 weeks, longer if umbilicate lichens are used (see below)
Asia, southern Europe	orchil	*Roccella*†	lecanoric	3 weeks§

*The primary lichen used, but see also p. 11.
**Most lichens contain several acids: Chart 5a, p. 48.
†Genuine orchil contains only *Roccella* (see Chart 2a, p. 17).
§Timing: the only 3-week AM dye is orchil; all other AM dyes require 16–18 weeks.

European AM Dyes

Dyes based on *Ochrolechia tartarea* are made the same way as orsallia, but the orcein develops in less time (Chart 3b). However, unlike leathery umbilicate lichens, *Ochrolechia* crumbles into pieces, so when prepar-ing cudbear and korkje vats, add just enough water and ammonia to barely cover the lichens. Otherwise, prepare the dye bath the same as or-sallia (p. 26). If you follow the historical precedent, however, and com-bine umbilicate lichens with *O. tartarea*, adjust the vat timing somewhere between 2 and 4 months. (If this is successful, you can experiment with a shorter fermentation period, but in my opinion, longer is always better.)

Natural (and Unnatural) Materials

Almost any natural or manmade fibre can be dyed with lichens, includ-ing alpaca, angora, cashmere, cotton, dog hair, linen, mohair, Orlon, quivet, rayon, silk and wool, in addition to paper fibres and anything synthetic. Manufactured textiles of any fibre can be lichen-dyed; try rib-bon, lace eyelet and other garment trims. Previously dyed yarns can be over-dyed with lichens; this includes failed natural dye experiments using other dyestuffs. Cane, reed, ramie, basketry fibres, feathers, leather and handmade papers are suitable, as are hair and hide, marble, wood and veneer, grasses and dried flowers. Eggs, bones, and buttons (even plastic ones) can be lichen-dyed, too. One of my successes is my lichen-dyed Tilly hat, which, in spite of repeated exposure to direct sunlight, re-mained purple, in my daughter's opinion, for too long a time. You can also dye purchased clothing such as lingerie.

Lichens are used to colour food. In India and Saudi Arabia, lichens add colour and texture to rice and grain dishes; authentic garam masala con-tains lichens. *Lecanora esculenta* was the Biblical "manna" that "dropped" from heaven, although a more plausible scenario involves a terricolous substrate from which lichens loosen in high winds. Some hennas contain lichens (including the American product Coloura) and they are essential in manufacturing cosmetics such as perfume. Lichens add flavor, colour and texture to bread. Lichen tonics are illustrated in Richardson 1988 and 1991, and homeopathic lichen-based treatments are common today in North America.

Fibre Preparation

Many disappointing dye results—including poor colour absorption and fading—can be traced to fibre preparation. Wool is the easiest fibre to handle, but raw fleece is the most laborious to prepare for dyeing. Wash first (twice, if it's dirty) in warm, soapy water. All soap must be rinsed away before dyeing fleece. Don't trust just one rinse to remove all suds; if in doubt, repeat this step.

Bronson's recipe for scouring wool (circa 1817) begins: "To one barrel of urine add one bushel of hog dung." Fortunately, things have changed. Simply soak wool in warm water for 1–2 hours before dyeing. Treat hand-spun weaving and knitting fibres of cotton and blends to a 4-hour pre-soak before dyeing. If using commercially spun yarn, a soapy wash is essential before the pre-dye soak to remove sizing and other chemicals that your eye does not necessarily "see." (Tip: sniff the yarn.) Rinse the yarn in cooler water, then pre-soak for dyeing in the usual way. It is as important to pay attention to how you handle fibre before and after dyeing as it is to worry about what happens in the dye pot. The most experienced dyers understand this point and they never take short cuts at this stage of the process.

Wind yarn into a skein before dyeing. Use a niddy noddy (see Glossary) or the back of a chair. Skeins with a large diameter dye more evenly and dry more quickly. There's a tendency among some spinners to wind small-diameter skeins, which I refer to as "dye pot donuts"; these swell when wet so that the dye cannot penetrate. Tie skeins with six to eight loose figure 8's. Usemore ties for fine or hairy yarns such as mohair, slippery fibres or singles. Extra ties preventing tangling and save time in the long run.

To dye resistant fibres (basketry, buttons, leather, plastic and wood), soak first in boiling water (if the material can take this treatment; otherwise, use hot water). Make sure items to be dyed are free of dust. Some materials (feathers, fur) dye best in a solar bath (p. 38). A solar oven to use for outdoor dyeing, instead of a stove, is described on p. 21 of Jenny Dean's *Wild Colour*.

Equipment

Thrift shops and yard sales have pots, buckets, strainers and cups, which are all the novice needs, but you must never use dye equipment for cooking food. Start with a pot that holds 9 l (2 gal). Enamel pots are fine, but stainless steel is the best investment (mine have had two decades of use). Pots must have a lid that fits. (Dilute ammonia in AM baths is not harmful, but I always keep dye pots covered.) Other useful equipment includes a wooden spoon, glass measuring cup, apron and pot holders. I personally use heavy-duty rubber gloves lined with cotton. To test dye-bath pH (p. 44), litmus paper is essential. No equipment is more useful than two or three pails and a few plastic strainers (colanders) that fit exactly on top of the pails, leaving your hands free. Spinners love to cram the dye pot. But did you realize that fleece absorbs *twice as much dye* as yarn? If you use pantyhose or muslin bags to contain fleece in the dye pot, these "bags" will absorb dye—dye you want on the fibre. Use mesh lingerie bags instead.

Light Fastness and Delayed Rinsing

There is a direct connection between proper rinsing and fastness. Some books suggest rinsing dyed fibres immediately. But with lichen-dyed fibres, it is essential to cool the yarn first. Lichen-dyed fibres are more fast if they are not rinsed for at least 24 hours: this stabilizes the dye and prevents after-dye run off. Here is my technique for delayed rinsing: first, leave the fibre in the AM or BWM dye bath to cool for 24 hours. Then, remove the fibre, place it in a colander over a pail and leave it another 24 hours. (What you collect can be reused.) After two days, rinse the fibre (which may be completely dry) in cold water. Even with dark colours, there will be very little dye run off, and your reward is improved fastness.

Exposing lichen-dyed fibres to full sunlight (Casselman 1992c) is considered heretical, for AM lichen dyes are said to "fade before your very eyes." But I routinely dry my orsallia-dyed yarn outdoors (and wear my lichen-dyed hat) with little noticeable fading.

Troubleshooting

Good technique makes good dyes. Any lichen dye bath will produce colour, so "failure" means you are disappointed with the result. Maybe you were impatient (see Chart 3b, p. 27)? Did you use too much fibre (p. 45)? Have you used the right method (see Chart 3a, p. 26, and C test, p. 49)? Did you wash the lichens first? Older books include this step, but washing lichens can rinse away valuable dye substances. Did you heat the dye too briefly? BWM baths need long, slow processing (p. 25). Did the colour wash out or fade? Use the post-dye rinse (see above).

In my experience, most AM dye problems begin with vat preparation. AM dyes require more patience than BWM dyes. It helps if your first vat is a small one: tending a small vat is more likely to inspire confidence than fretting over a massive one that is wasteful if it fails to provide the expected results. I recommend glass for the vat, and make sure the lid is tight. If you must pad the lid, use plastic kitchen wrap instead of wax paper. Never substitute industrial-strength ammonia. (Industrial ammonia is *30 times stronger* than the household variety.) If you can't find household ammonia, substitute window-cleaning liquid.

Lack of aeration causes some AM vats to fail. Shake much more often if the colour does not start to shift within 2 weeks (p. 27). If the colour does not shift within 3 weeks, do not add more ammonia. Additional ammonia will not rescue a vat that has been neglected or kept too cool. Instead, move the vat into direct sunlight and shake vigorously 10–12 times a day for 3–4 days. Unless dyeing resistant fibres (p. 29), avoid placing fibre directly in the AM vat; make up a dye bath as on p. 27. Ideal vat temperature is between 10°C (50°F) and 25°C (80°F). Vats ignored (relegated to cold cellars or garages) may not develop properly, nor will vats left unattended on hot patios. Do not shorten the fermentation: if in doubt, wait.

CHARTS 3c AND 3d: INTERNATIONAL LICHEN DYES

Symbols: * indicates that the most current names for these species can be found in Brodo, Sharnoff and Sharnoff (North America); Purvis et al. (UK); Jahns (Europe). ** indicates lichen name misspelled in source cited, but corrected here. "Pers. comm." refers to tests accompanied by dyed samples, now in my personal collection (see Acknowledgements). Additional symbols and notes are on pp. 34 and 36.

Ethical dyes: You can mix and match AM and BWM lichens. See p. 26.

CHART 3c: 80 INTERNATIONAL AM AND POD LICHEN DYES

AM lichens used	Colour/results	Source
Actinogyra muehlenbergii	various	Casselman 1986–1994
Actinogyra muehlenbergii	pink, rose	pers. comm., Stone
Agrophora lyngei	brownish-violet	McGrath
Alectoria sarmentosa	taupe-violet	pers. comm., Sherrodd
Baeomyces fungoides	pale salmon	Milner
Bryoria fremontii	green	Brough 1984
Caloplaca trachyphylla	red-purple	Brough 1988
Cetraria cucullata	plum	McGrath
Cetraria delisei	fuchsia	Chambers in Buchanan
Cetraria islandica	red	Swenson in Weigle 1973
Cetraria islandica	rusty brown	McGrath
Cetraria nivilis	violet	Llano 1944
Cladonia impexa*	pink	Robertson
Coccotrema maritimum	olive (plus mordant§)	pers. comm., Sherrodd
Cornicularia californica	light brown	Brough 1984
Dactylina arctica	fuchsia	Chambers in Buchanan
Diploschistes scruposus*	red	Aiken
Diploschistes spp.	red, purple	Kok
Evernia prunastri	pink	Fraser

CHART 3c: (cont.)

AM lichens used	Colour/results	Source
Evernia prunastri	brownish-violet	Grierson 1986
Evernia spp.	green	Yacopino in Weigle 1973
*Gyrophora deusta**	various	Westring 1805
Gyrophora spp.	various	Gerber and Gerber
Haematomma lapponicum	purple-red	Padgham in Bliss
Haematomma ventosum	deep magenta	Grierson 1984
*Isidium westringii**	orange-pink	Westring 1805
Lasallia papulosa	various	Casselman 1978–80
Lasallia papulosa	pink	McGuffin
Lasallia pustulata	red	pers. comm., Carlyon
*Lecanora pallescens**	various	Hoad
*Lecanora tartarea**	red	Edmondston
Lobaria spathulata§	reddish range	Teramura 1984§
*Melanelia glabratula**	fuchsia	pers. comm., Upton
Nephroma helveticum	dark brown	Brough 1984
Ochrolechia parella	wine red	Goodwin
Ochrolechia parella	plum	Simmons
Ochrolechia tartarea	pink, fuchsia	pers. comm., Almedal
Ochrolechia tartarea	blue-purple	Bolton
Ochrolechia tartarea	red	Mitchell
Ochrolechia tartarea	violet-red	Høiland
Ochrolechia tartarea	red-violet	Sandberg and Sisefsky
Ochrolechia tartarea	purple	Wickens
Ochrolechia spp.	various	Bærentsen
Omphalodiscus virginis	various	McGrath
Parmelia fuliginosa	violet-purple	Bolton
*Parmelia glabratula**	grey-red	Grierson 1986
*Parmelia perlata**	bright pink, magenta	Grae
*Parmelia pertusa**	pink, red	Robertson
Parmelia reticulata	dusty pink, bright pink	Milner
*Parmelia ulophyllodes** **	various reds	Aiken
Parmotrema perforatum	various reds	pers. comm., Gerber
Parmotrema tinctorum	various reds	pers. comm., Clements
Parmotrema tinctorum‡	various reds	Teramura 1984
Peltigera aphthosa	pink	pers. comm., Sherrodd
Peltigera aphthosa	pink	Windt
Peltigera venosa	pink-grey, purple	Brough 1984
*Pertusaria corralina**	red-purple	Grierson 1986
Placopsis gelida	various	pers. comm., Roubal
Pseudevernia consocians	pink	Shag Rag Weavers
Pseudocyphellaria coronata	various	Milner

CHART 3c: (cont.)

AM lichens used	Colour/results	Source
*Pseudocyphellaria crocata**	various	Gordon
Pseudocyphellaria spp.	orange	Yacopino in Weigle 1973
*Punctelia rudecta**	pink	pers. comm., Marr
Ramalina farinacea	brownish-pink	Brough 1984
Ramalina scopulorum	red	Bolton
Ramalina spp.	post-dye treatment	Hofmann
Roccella babingtonii	deep purple	Perkins
Roccella fuciformis	crimson, purple	Llano 1944
Roccella montagnei	purple	Casselman 1992
Roccella phycopsis	crimson, purple	Llano 1944
Roccella tinctoria	purple	Perkins
Sphaerophorus spp.*	red	Lindsay 1854
*Teloschistes velifera***	pink, purple, slate blue	Milner
*Umbilicaria americana**	various	Casselman 1994
Umbilicaria deusta	various	Casselman 1978–1980
Umbilicaria hyperborea	various	Casselman 1986
Umbilicaria mammulata	various	Casselman 1980
*Umbilicaria muehlenbergii**	various	Casselman 1978–1980
*Umbilicaria papulosa**	various	Casselman 1978
*Umbilicaria papulosa**	magenta	Milner
Umbilicaria pensylvanica	various	Hewitt in Weigle 1973
Umbilicaria phaea	various	pers. comm., Brough
Umbilicaria polyphylla	various	Casselman 1986
Umbilicaria polyrrhiza	various	Casselman 1986
Umbilicaria proboscidea	various	Casselman 1986
*Umbilicaria pustulata**	purple	Grierson 1986
*Umbilicaria pustulata**	various	Lindsay 1856
*Umbilicaria pustulata**	various	Sandberg and Sisefsky
Umbilicaria torrefacta	various	Casselman 1986
*Umbilicaria vellea**	various	Casselman 1994b
Umbilicaria spp.	various	Aiken
Umbilicaria spp.	various	Gerber and Gerber
Umbilicaria spp.	various	Weigle 1974
*Urceolaria scruposa**	cherry	Lindsay 1854
*Usnea barbata**	purple	Sauvé
*Usnea glabrata** ‡	green-greyish-brown	Brough 1984
*Usnea hirta***	purple	Robertson
Usnea spp.	purple	McGrath
*Variolaria lactea**	pink	Westring 1805
*Variolaria orcina**	purple	Bancroft
Xanthoparmelia conspersa	drab apricot	Milner

CHART 3c: (cont.)

AM lichens used	Colour/results	Source
*Xanthoria ectanea**	POD blue, slate blue	pers. comm., Moroney
Xanthoria ectanoides	POD blue	pers. comm., Upton
Xanthoria elegans	POD blue/mauve	pers. comm., Bryant
Xanthoria parietina	POD blue	Bærentsen
Xanthoria parietina	POD blue	Bolton
Xanthoria parietina	POD violet	Grierson
Xanthoria polycarpa	POD blue	Brough 1988
Xanthoria polycarpa	POD pink/blue	pers. comm., Park
Xanthoria spp.	POD blue	Windt

Notes: *Actinogyra, Gyrophora* and *Lasallia* are synonyms for certain species of *Umbilicaria* (e.g., the North American lichen *Lasallia papulosa* and the chemically similar European species *Lasallia pustulata* were formerly named *Umbilicaria*).

The date following an author's name (e.g., Brough 1988) indicates that more than one article or book by this source is in the Bibliography.

"Spp." = species, collectively, of this or any other genus.

CHART 3d: 70 INTERNATIONAL BWM LICHEN DYES

BWM lichens	Colour	Source
Alectoria spp.	bright orange	Windt
Bryoria fremontii	tan-brown	Brough 1984
Bryoria fuscescens	yellow	Grierson 1986
Candelariella vitellina	yellow	Brough 1988
Cetraria canadensis	greenish-yellow	Lewis in Bliss
Cetraria ericetorum	maize, tan	Teramura 1992
Cetraria islandica	brown	Bolton
Cetraria islandica	yellow, brown	Goubitz
Cetraria islandica	yellow	McGuffin
Cetraria islandica	brown	Lindsay 1856
Cetraria tilesii	bright yellow	Chambers in Buchanan
*Cladonia alpestris**	yellow	Casselman 1980
Cladonia cristatella	light green	pers. comm., Becker
*Cladonia portentosa**	leaf green	Grierson 1986
Cladonia pyxidata	gold	McGuffin
*Cladonia rangiferina**	red-brown	Fraser
*Cladonia rangiferina**	brown	Bächi-Nussbaumer
Cornicularia divergens	orange	McGrath
Dermatocarpon miniatum	brown-olive	Brough 1988

CHART 3d: (cont.)

BWM lichens	Colour	Source
Evernia prunastri	light orange	Grierson 1986
*Haematomma ventosa**	chocolate brown	Bolton
*Haematomma ventosa**	red-brown	Lye and Lye
Hypogymnia physodes	gold, orange-brown	Bolton
Hypogymnia physodes	green (plus mordant[§])	Hoad
Hypogymnia physodes	tan, warm brown	Ploss
Lecanora muralis	tawny olive	Brough 1988
Letharia columbiana	yellow	Brough 1984
Letharia vulpina	yellow	Bearfoot
Letharia spp.	brilliant yellow	Windt
Lobaria pulmonaria	apricot, orange, rust	pers. comm., Dowd
Lobaria pulmonaria	gold, rust, brown	pers. comm., Ouderman
Lobaria pulmonaria	red-brown	Rutty
Lobaria pulmonaria	reddish-brown	Sandberg and Sisefsky
Lobaria pulmonaria	orange	Thurston
*Melanelia stygia**	tan to brown	Solberg
Nephroma expallidum	brown	McGrath
Nephroma helveticum	orange-brown	Brough 1984
Parmelia arnoldii	gold	Mustard
*Parmelia caperata**	yellow	Mustard
Parmelia clavulifera	copper, rust	Teramura 1984
*Parmelia olivacea**	tan to brown	Solberg
Parmelia omphalodes	orange-brown	Bærentsen
Parmelia omphalodes	orange-rust	Bolton
Parmelia omphalodes	strong red-brown	Davenport
Parmelia omphalodes	rust	Grierson 1986
Parmelia omphalodes	red-brown	Lindsay 1856
Parmelia omphalodes	rusty red	Milner
Parmelia omphalodes	orange-brown	Thurston
*Parmelia rudecta**	yellow, gold, brown	pers. comm., Marr
Parmelia saxatilis	brownish-red	Mitchell in Schetky
Parmelia saxatilis	bronze	Sauvé
Parmelia saxatilis	brown	van de Vrande
Parmelia saxatilis	orange (plus mordant[§])	van Stralen
Parmelia saxatilis	reddish-brown	Wickens
Parmelia sulcata	reddish-brown	Aiken
Parmotrema tinctorum[‡]	gold	Teramura 1984
Peltigera canina	yellow	Wold and Nielsen
Peltigera spp.	yellow-tan (plus mordant[§])	Furry and Viemont
Peltigera spp.	rose-tan (plus mordant[§])	Krochmal and Krochmal
Pertusaria coriacea	dark brown	McGrath

CHART 3d: (cont.)

BWM lichens	Colour	Source
Physcia spp.	yellow	Casselman 1991
Platismatia glauca	orange-tan	Lindsay 1854
Platismatia glauca	apricot yellow	Grierson 1986
Pseudevernia consocians **	orange	Shag Rag Weavers
Pseudevernia furfuracea	vivid orange	Grierson 1986
Pseudocyphellaria anomala	orange-brown	Brough 1984
Pseudocyphellaria coronata	various	Lloyd
Pseudocyphellaria crocata	various	Gordon
Ramalina scopulorum	yellow	pers. comm., Kilbride
Ramalina spp.	yellow	Antúnez de Mayolo
Ramalina spp.	post-dye treatment	Hofmann
Stereocaulon spp.	orange, rust	McGrath
Teloschistes flavicans	yellow-orange	Antúnez de Mayolo
Umbilicaria spp.	chocolate brown	pers. comm., Grude
Umbilicaria spp.	brown, brownish-green	Lindsay 1856
*Usnea articulata**	rich ochre-gold (plus mordant[§])	Davenport
Usnea barbata[‡]	blue	Antúnez de Mayolo
*Usnea dayspoga**	orange-brown	Brough 1984
*Usnea dayspoga**	red-brown	Lye and Lye
Usnea diffracta	green (plus mordant[§])	Teramura 1984
Usnea rubescens	gold-orange	Teramura 1992
Usnea subfloridana	greyish-olive	Grierson 1986
Usnea spp.	yellow, orange	Westring 1805
*Xanthoparmelia centrifuga**	tan to brown	Solberg
*Xanthoparmelia conspersa**	reddish-brown	pers. comm., Hopkins
Xanthoparmelia lineola	russet	Brough 1988
Xanthoparmelia taractica	copper	McGuffin
Xanthoparmelia spp.	yellow, gold, brown	Casselman 1994
Xanthoria parietina[‡]	corn yellow	Grierson 1986
Xanthoria spp.	orange	Rutt

Symbols: [‡]Some sources use two dye methods with the same lichen: see Teramura (pp. 25, 30). Others are Antúnez de Mayolo; and Grierson's BWM treatment of *Xanthoria*, which is normally a POD dye (Chart 3a, p. 27).

[§]AM and BWM lichens are substantive dyestuffs that do not require mordants. Some authors do use mordants, but colours can be changed using alternatives (Chart 4, p. 43) and/or pH adjustment (p. 45). Mordants pose a health risk if not used with care, and they can damage yarn. Alternative additives are products deemed safe under normal household use.

4

Eco Dyes and Alternative Mordants

Dyes that are safe for the environment are also safer for the dyer. About a decade ago, I began, for reasons of health, to focus on safer work methods. Coincidental with concerns for personal safety were issues involving ethics. Should we exploit, for dyeing, specific botanical organisms within ecosystems that are already under pressure (see Casselman 1992a, 1992b, 1993b, 1994b)? As I grappled with these questions, I also began to develop more ecologically sound and ethical methodologies. The name "Eco Dyes" was formalized when I presented a program by that name at a 1995 Colorado forum on natural dyes.

Eco Dyes is a philosophy directed toward preventing problems that must later be solved: for example, if you don't use the chemical mordants associated with natural dyes, there is no disposal problem. And if you collect "found" lichens when out walking and hiking, there's no need for group collecting, which tends to put too much pressure on specific species. The Eco Dye philosophy is based on salvage botany (p. 47), but it goes beyond nature to include craft techniques such as exhaust dyes, solar dyes and alternative mordants. Every aspect of the Eco Dye philosophy is applicable to lichen dyes. Waste is further avoided when you collect according to established international guidelines (see Code of Ethics, p. 47).

Reduced Ammonia AM Dye Formula

The amount of ammonia in the vat ratio described on page 26 can be reduced. For those who may be sensitive to ammonia, here is a 1:3 formula that uses a lesser amount.

1. Prepare the AM vat as far as placing the lichens in an appropriately

sized jar (p. 26). Next, pour undiluted household ammonia over the lichens, enough to barely cover the pieces (measure or estimate amount used: see step 2, below). Close the vat tightly. Shake vigorously and set aside for 2–3 days.

2. Remove the vat lid. Add 3 times as much water as ammonia. Replace the lid. Shake the vat vigourously several times a day. Let the vat sit another 15 weeks (Chart 3b, p. 27).

3. Pour off the dye liquor and dilute it with water to make the dye bath. Use as on p. 27 (or below).

Three-Step Solar Lichen Dyes

1. Prepare the AM vat as usual (p. 26 or the 1:3 formula above) and age the vat the required time (Chart 3b, p. 27). (Shorten this step and you diminish colour diversity and compromise fastness.)

2. Pour off 250 ml (1 c) of vat liquor. In a large glass or Pyrex dish, dilute the vat liquor with 4 parts water. Now, add 28 g (1 oz) prepared fibre and cover the dish tightly with plastic wrap.

3. Place the dish in direct sunlight. A greenhouse, a sunny window or a concrete patio is usually hot enough; you can also devise a solar oven (see p. 30). Leave the fibre in the dye for about 8 days; remove and rinse (p. 30). **Caution:** in some climates, such as Australia and the American southwest, the heat is too intense for solar-oven dyeing with lichens; never allow AM dyes in particular to exceed the temperatures on page 27.

Three-Step POD Lichen Dyes

Ephemeral blue dyes (and a menstrual tea: see Epilogue) can be made from common orange lichens (*Xanthoria* spp., Chart 3c, p. 31). Why bother with colours that are not fast, you may ask? POD dyes are an exercise in investigative dyeing; they require patience, but it is time well-spent to see pink dyes photo-oxidize to blue. But POD dyes are satisfactory if you know how the yarn you dye will be used (e.g., your own garments). POD dyes are also useful for greens (p. 46). But the most persuasive reason to try POD dyes is abundance. Worldwide, *Xanthoria* spp. are "weedy" in rural and urban settings. As for fastness, the fading of murex did nothing to diminish its cultural value for 3,000 years. Why apply a different performance standard to POD dyes?

POD dyes involve 3 steps: 1. vat preparation; 2. dyeing; 3. photo-oxidization.

1. Half-fill a 500 ml (2 c) jar with 250 ml (1 c) crumbled *Xanthoria*. You can use any species; see Chart 3c, p. 31. Moisten the lichens with 125 ml (½ c) household ammonia; stir, replace the lid and wait 2 days. Then add 375 ml (1½ c) water: use enough to make a soupy "porridge." Stir vigourously. Replace the lid. After 3 weeks, the colour will shift to pink; wait another 6–8 weeks.

2. Strain off the vat liquor; add sufficient water to make a bath. Place 28 g (1 oz) prepared fibre in the dye bath and heat to 82°C (180°F). Maintain temperature 20 minutes, reduce heat and process an hour, or until the fibre is dyed pink. (The stronger the pink, the better your blue will be: p. 46.)

3. Remove the fibre, squeeze out the moisture and place the damp yarn in direct sunlight. Turn the yarn over frequently. As it dries, the colour will shift to blue. (At first, the yarn will look greyish—don't be discouraged!) Keep *re-wetting* the fibre in the dye bath. Cloudy weather? Return the fibre to the dye and continue another day. Rinse as on p. 30.

Fastness and Exhaust Dyes

Some AM and BWM baths have enough pigment for several exhausts. The first yarn you place in a bath absorbs most of the dye; the second batch of yarn dyed is the "exhaust." Exhaust dyeing is a routine procedure, but like solar dyes, colours from exhausts may not be as fast as from "first dips." To remove fibre from a dye bath after only a few minutes of dyeing (no matter how much you like the colour) is an invitation to fading. Try these ideas instead.

1. Good exhausts come from strong dye baths (p. 46). If you start with magenta or purple from your first AM dip, successive exhausts will provide good colours. With AM dyes, if the vat is not properly prepared, if the orcein is underdeveloped due to improper timing (p. 12) or if you have used too much yarn, the dye bath will not provide satisfactory exhausts.

2. Aim for maximum contrast between first dip and exhaust colours. Try this: for the first dip, use ⅓ of the total weight of the fibre you wish to dye; save ⅔ of your fibre for the exhaust dip.

3. Avoid using a small amount of dyestuff to make pastels. A more successful technique is to "cram" the exhaust of a strong dye bath. If your first dip yields magenta and you use twice as much fibre in the exhaust, you will naturally get a lighter shade.

4. Cramming a BWM dye bath can be unproductive. Here is an alternative method: do a test sequence by putting 28 g (1 oz) of fibre in the dye pot every 30 minutes for 2 hours or for as long as it takes to absorb the available pigment. (See also p. 46.)

5. Exhausts can be made from replenished AM vats. In a clean jar, cover the used lichen pieces with warm water and set aside another 4 weeks. (There's no point adding more ammonia because the fermentation is over.) Note: colours from replenished vats are not as fast or as intense.

Washing Dyed Fibres

There is no need to wash what is not dirty. The obsession with washing natural-dyed fibre is energy that is better directed, in my opinion, to more careful fibre preparation (p. 28). Just as there is no reason whatsoever to wash lichens (see p. 30), why wash lichen-dyed fibre? It makes more sense to take the time to give yarn an extra wash before dyeing. And whether the finished product is knitted, woven, hooked or quilted, it is far more important to pay attention to proper rinsing than to focus on post-dye washing.

This is why: to subject a splendid fuchsia or magenta to the rigors of even "wool safe" soap is tocompromise fastness. Unbonded dye pigment will attach to the soap molecules and vanish down the drain with the suds. There are always some unbonded dye molecules present in fibre, but these nonetheless contribute to the finished colour. Too many unbonded dye molecules will cause "crocking"; the normal amount will not, provided you have carefully rinsed the fibre after dyeing. And even pH-neutral soap can shift or change AM and POD dye colours.

There is a time to wash lichen-dyed fibre and that is after the garment or weaving project is completed, by which time colours have "cured." I machine-wash (delicate cycle) my handwoven blankets, in which white threads are next to AM purples, to no ill effect. I do not wash because the fabric is dirty. There are other reasons—reasons many weavers, knitters and stitchers ignore. One is to "full" the finished fabric (to shrink it slightly to raise the nap); and another is because nothing knitted, woven or stitched is properly finished until it has been washed and/or pressed. For it is the final finishing that characterizes the outstanding handmade textile.

Lichens as Mordants

Lichens are substantive dyes. Mordants are not required (p. 36), but certain additives (e.g., ammonia) are part of the lichen-dye process.

Household products such as salt, vinegar and ammonia (Chart 4, p. 43) can increase dye uptake and improve fastness. Urine was used for this purpose and as a dye bath. This description is evocative: "At four in the afternoon three hogshead of urine were put into the copper [sic]. The urine cast up a thick scum, which was taken out with a broom . . ." (Bemiss). While we enjoy these colourful accounts, most dyers admit they have never actually tried urine. Dyeing with "your own urine" (or what in 1995 I dubbed "Y/O/U") is an adventure, but more importantly, one way to verify historical dye practices that we read about, yet never try.

Another historical use of lichens is as a mordant (see Hofmann, p. 36). For obvious reasons, only common or weedy species should be used for this purpose, which is one way to investigate the other properties of lichen substances. Note: I use as mordants only those species that yield little colour on their own; these are shades that dyers jokingly refer to as "warm beige" or "champagne." In North America the most appropriate species to use as mordants are abundant lichens such as *Hypogymnia*, *Platismatia*, and *Usnea*. Few of these genera in my region produce outstanding BWM colours. This may not be the case where you live: consult the sources cited in Charts 3c and 3d (pp. 31, 34) and your field guide (p. 52).

I simply collect fallen lichens on my daily walks. Store them until you have enough to try. Because the concentration of acid varies from one species to another, your lichen mordants will reflect the subtleties and nuances unique to your personal mixture.

Very few lichens are required to make an experimental mordant bath. I suggest starting with perhaps a plastic bread bag full of lichens, processed in approximately 2–4 l (2–4 qt) of water. Bring the lichens and water to a boil, then reduce the heat and simmer for 1 hour. Strain off the liquid; use a fairly fine mesh strainer (rather than a colander) to trap any small pieces. Discard the used lichens. For pre-mordanted fibre, prepare ½k (17–18 oz) of yarn by pre-soaking (see p. 29). Immerse the wet fibre in cooled lichen liquor. (The liquor from some species will form a loose gel when cooled—rather like a soft pudding. If this happens, heat will reconstitute the bath. Bring the mordant bath to a bare simmer (see p. 27). Leave the fibre in the bath overnight to cool completely. There is no need to wash the yarn (see p. 30). But if some lichen pieces remain attached to the yarn, shake the skeins vigorously or use my ploy, which is to whack them against the deck.

Try experimenting with lichen-based mordants as a base for subsequent over-dyeing with BWM species that contain strong tinctorial substances (e.g., *Parmelia saxatilis* or *Xanthoparmelia* spp.). This "lichen/lichen" method of mordanting/dyeing has several benefits: first,

the actual dye bath in which you process the lichen-mordanted yarn requires fewer dye lichens; and second, there is a wonderful aroma (p. 17)
that lingers when you over-dye lichen-mordanted fibres with another
natural dye (e.g., try top-dyeing odoriferous indigo). (See Acknowledgements.)

Found Materials and Household Mordants

The conventional mordants associated with natural dyeing are alum (alu-
minum potassium sulphate); chrome (potassium dichromate); copper
(copper sulphate); iron (ferrous sulphate); and tin (stannous chloride).On
a personal level, I made the decision a few years ago to stop using chrome
and I have not since changed my mind about the potential health risks associated with this mordant. (I have similar concerns about industrial-
strength ammonia: see p. 30). As noted on page 36, lichen dyes are substantive and do not require mordants.

But if you want to try mordants to vary colour, I suggest you focus attention on "found" materials and household products. Scrap metal, iron,
steel wool and copper pipe are effective, as is sheet tin (the so-called "tin
can" is not tin, but an alloy). Where all substitute mordants are con-
cerned, pick and choose the products you feel safe with; a case in point is
household cleaning products. Glass or window cleaner is a weak ammonia substitute, but it also contains other chemicals to which you may be
sensitive. Mold and mildew removers are my favorite post-dye treatments: when you randomly spray an AM-dyed fabric or yarn with a dilute solution (half product, half water), the pH shift that occurs when the
substitute mordant comes into contact with the dyed textile, produces attractive patterns of variegation.

The use of the dye pot *itself* as a mordant is controversial. Some sources
claim this technique does not work, but personally, I find that antique
brass, copper, iron and tin pots do produce effective colours—especially
bronze, rust, copper and olive. (As evidence, see the colour photograph
showing this method in my 1997 *SSD* article.) Many books advise dyers
not to use chipped pots, but in my experience, damaged pots can create
interesting effects. Try this: tie some pennies in a mesh bag and place atop
yarn in a damaged dye pot. Barely cover the fibre (and pennies) with
water. Heat the dye bath. (You are actually steaming the fibre.) Pot-as-
mordant methodologies, substitute mordants and intuitive techniques
are also the focus of current thesis research in Australia (see
Acknowledgements). Outstanding references on traditional colonial mordants are Adrosko and Liles; both include comprehensive lists which include chemical formulas.

CHART 4: ADDITIVES AND ALTERNATIVE MORDANTS

Product	Dye type	Effect	How to use
aluminum pot	AM, BWM	shifts colour	dye pot
ammonia*	BWM	aids BWM extraction	pre-dye soak
baking soda	AM, POD	makes yarn harsh: use not recommended	
brass§	AM, BWM, POD	shifts colour	bath additive
brass, pot	BWM	increases yellow	dye pot
chalk*	AM	increases pH (more alkaline)	bath additive
coins	AM, BWM	for special effects, see p. 43	
copper§	AM, BWM	shifts colour	bath additive
copper, pot	BWM	increases green/olive	dye pot
dye pot	AM, BWM	for special effects, use chipped pot: see p. 42	
glass cleaner	AM, POD	shifts pH	post-dye treatment
iron, pot	BWM	darkens colour	dye pot
iron, "tea"	AM, BWM	darkens colour	post-dye treatment
lichens	BWM	provides pale ground colour	pre-mordant
liquid drain cleaner	AM, BWM	for special effects, see p. 43	reagent for testing lichens
onion, skins	AM, BWM	increases yellow: over-dye	bath additive
rhubarb, leaves	BWM	increases yellow: over-dye	pre-mordant
salt**	AM, BWM, POD	improves fastness	bath additive
soda, caustic and washing	AM	increases pH†	bath additive
sumac	BWM	increases yellow: over-dye	bath additive
tin§	AM, BWM	intensifies colour	bath additive
tin, pot	AM, BWM	intensifies colour	dye pot
urine	AM, POD	increases dye uptake	pre-dye soak
vinegar**	AM	lowers pH (more acidic)	bath additive
vinegar**	AM, BWM	shifts colour	pre- or post-dye treatment

Symbols: * 10 ml (2 tsp) per 58 g (2 oz) fibre; ** use any amount; † Grierson adds soda ash (sodium carbonate) to AM dyes but there are other ways (p. 44) to increase dye-bath pH; §scrap metal, brass/copper pipe, etc.

Note: products sold for household use are here described as "safe"; for instance, bleach or Clorox (sodium hypochlorite), used for C test, p. 49. Some sources (e.g., McGrath) use industrial strength ammonia, which I do not recommend (p. 30). Vinegar (dilute acetic acid) varies in strength from 3% (USA) to 5% (Canada, UK, Australia); 7% is sold as "pickling" vinegar.

The key to spectacular results with variegated yarn is to avoid handling or moving the fibre until it is completely *dry*. Carefully lift the fibre into a colander (don't move it about or you could lose the variegation).

Let the fibre sit another 1–2 days. The only time you need to follow Eco Dyeing with a soapy rinse is if you use rusty iron, which, I admit, is messy. One solution is the "iron tea" recommended by authors such as Jenny Dean (*Wild Colour*) and Jim Liles (*Art and Craft of Natural Dyeing*), who soak scrap iron in vinegar, then strain off this "iron tea" for use as a mordant. However, I would not heat such a solution (that is, add it to a dye bath). I suggest it be used without heat, only as a pre-dye soak or a post-dye treatment.

My students have produced exciting patterns by wrapping lingerie (*shibori*-fashion) around a metal object before dyeing the entire "bundle." Horseshoes can also be used this way. Try chalk or shells (whole or crumbled), or use stick deodorant as a resist (you can "paint" it on or remove it from the container and wrap the fabric around the entire stick). Powdered dye bath additives (e.g., salt, soda) are first dissolved in boiling water. You can also spritz mordant solutions (e.g., vinegar) on dry yarn prior to dyeing and use ties or elastics to create resist patterns.

How to Adjust AM Dye Bath pH

AM dye shades vary widely: typical colours include pink, rose, crimson, magenta, purple and violet (see Chart 3c, p. 31). (Additional colour illustrations relevant to pH adjustment are included in my articles: see p. 56.) One of the persistent myths about AM dyes is the notion that mordants or additives must be used to vary colours. This is not necessarily the case. For example, it is entirely possible to obtain pink, rose, lavender, fuchsia and purple from the same dye bath without using any mordants whatsoever.

By adjusting the dye bath, it is possible to lower the pH (pH 3–7) to enhance reds or raise it (pH 8–12) to shift colours towards blue/purple. For a description of the pH scale, see Chapter Notes, p. 45. Avoid extremes! For example, colours adjusted below pH 3 may "brown out" and prove disappointing, and adjustment beyond pH 12 will impair the quality of the fibre. This is how to do it: let's say you've got violet and you prefer rose. The addition of vinegar to the actual dye bath or a post-dye treatment (e.g., a dip) will lower the pH and change the colour. You can also use a post-dye soak in vinegar. Tip: when you use vinegar as a post-dye treatment, you avoid contaminating the dye bath, which gives you an opportunity to subsequently explore other colour potential. But how much vinegar do you use?

Chemistry is the key. You need some pH test paper (see p. 46). Tear off two 2–3 cm (1 inch) strips of pH paper. Now pour a scant 25 ml (1 tbsp) of AM vat liquor into each of two small containers. Add a few drops of vinegar to one container and a similar amount of ammonia to the other. Dip one pH paper into one container and the other into the second container. (Don't saturate the paper, just get the tip wet.) Now compare the two pH readings with the colour chart provided with the papers. This exercise shows the extent to which you can shift the pH of the dye bath. You can also change the pH of AM dyed fibre after it has been dyed. By varying the amount of vinegar or ammonia in a post-dye rinse, you can very simply achieve a full range of AM dye colours, and without the use of soda. Dye a sample skein. If you like the colour, there's no need to adjust pH. If you want it lower, place the dyed skein (wet or dry) in a post-dye vinegar rinse (1:1 ratio of vinegar and water); alternatively, to increase pH, use a 1:20 solution of household ammonia to water.

Some dyers use soda to adjust pH (see Chart 4, p. 43). But because my AM method begins with a high pH vat, it is usually not necessary to increase pH in the dye bath. Here are some relevant pH measurements: the average orsallia dye vat has a pH of 11. The dye bath has a pH of 9–10. The reduced-ammonia dye bath (p. 37) is usually lower, approximately pH 8–9.

It is exciting to put fibre in a vinegar rinse and watch colours like magenta shift to deep rose. If you want the most attractive AM shades, begin with a strong AM dye bath. The stronger the dye bath (and the better the vat: i.e., good technique), the more you can manipulate dye-bath pH.

The most dramatic and intense AM dye colours are obtained from dye baths that have a pH of more than 10. But high pH *and* high temperature are a risky combination: you can ruin the yarn. The safest way to achieve these colours is to start with a maximum amount of dye liquor (500 ml, 2 c), diluted with 5 times as much water, and a small amount of fibre (56 g, 2 oz). Heat to 70°C (160°F) and maintain this temperature for 30 minutes. Remove the dye bath from the heat. Cool overnight. The next day, reheat the dye pot to 70°C again, and maintain this temperature for 15 minutes. Cool once more, and use the delayed rinse (p. 30). If the second and third colours are satisfactory, you can continue to exhaust the dye bath. Each colour will be slightly different, even if you do not adjust the pH, because the pH of AM dye baths lowers naturally as the dyeing progresses. But if you want pastels, after the first dip, cram the dye bath to absorb all of the pigment that remains.

CHAPTER NOTES

pH scale The pH scale is a convenient way to measure acidity and alkalinity. The scale ranges from pH 1 (highly acidic) to pH 14 (highly alkaline); pH 7 = neutral. The scale is logarithmic: pH 8 is weakly alkaline; pH 9 is 10 times more alkaline. But pH 10 is 100 times more alkaline than pH

8. Most AM vats are pH 9–11; after dilution with water, dye baths are generally pH 8–9. Strongly alkaline baths (above pH 11) damage wool, so avoid excessive heat (p. 45). Small containers of pH test paper are sold in rolls; full-range papers will measure pH 1–14. Other papers measure only part of the scale: e.g., pH 5–10. You can also use a pH meter, but these are expensive and often unreliable.

Dye-bath strength Less experienced dyers are surprised to learn that the amount of water used in a dye bath does not dilute dye bath intensity, or strength. It is the *weight of the fibre* that dilutes the amount of pigment in AM and BWM dye baths. This means that the more fibre you process in the first dip, the more you diminish the dyestuff. For example, 56 g (2 oz) of fibre processed in a strong BWM dye bath (from a species that yields orange-brown, for example) will produce an intense shade of rust; but 228 g (8 oz) of fibre processed in the same dye bath will produce only a warm tan. Be patient; use your first dip to explore the potential for strong colours; you can always add more yarn later (pp. 39–40).

Blue dyes from *Xanthoria* Expert POD blue dyers include Bærentsen (Færoe Islands), Moroney (Ireland), and Upton (Cornwall, England). These very experienced dyers obtain darker blues by re-dipping and re-oxidizing POD yarn, just like indigo. They also use POD blues as a ground colour for green (over-dyeing the blue with yellow). The history of POD dyes is somewhat confusing: Bolton and Upton are among sources that suggest POD dyes are fairly recent in origin. But in my research, I have traced blue dyes from *Xanthoria* as far back as the 18th century (Westring 1792 [in French], p. 24).

Sig, lit or Y/O/U. Urine is a natural compound; the commercial urea widely used in textile printing is a highly concentrated form. Ammonia develops as urine decomposes, hence the misconception that urine contains ammonia. Urine was a traditional dye additive used as a pre-dye treatment or, in some cases, as the actual dye bath liquid. Old recipes called for "stale urine," because decomposition increases the ammonia concentration. Poetic names for "chamber lye" include "lit" and "sig." The name I coined (Y/O/U: "your own urine") is consistent with the Eco Dye philosophy: most dyers are more comfortable experimenting with their *own*. Try this pre-dye treatment: place dry fibre in a zip-lock bag that contains 250 ml (1 c) Y/O/U; close the bag and place in the sun 1–2 days. My students at the 1998 Textile Fibre Forum in Australia did this, then used other Eco Dye techniques, with great success. Does the yarn smell after such a process? We got our answer when a workshop visitor inquired, "What smells *so good*?"

5

Ethics and Lichen Identification

Code of Ethics

Not only dyers use plants. Naturalists, teachers, herbalists and gardeners also collect plants for science, education, and recreation. Moreover, there is a considerable trade in lichens used as homeopathic treatments, wreaths, and cosmetics (see Epilogue), to which few in the anti-dye lobby have paid attention. But now there is an ethical way to gather plants. And better still, the international lichenological community has heard the message that dyers want to be part of the solution. "Salvage botany" is a way to collect dyeing flora that might otherwise be wasted.

Experts in Canada, the USA, the UK, and Australia have helped me devise this Code of Ethics:

1. Buy a field guide for your own geographic region (Chart 5b, p. 52); become informed as to how lichens reproduce. Understand lichen ecology and habitat issues.
2. Before you gather any lichens whatsoever, learn to identify five lichen species by their full Latin names.
3. Focus your attention only on "found" (unattached) lichens: see p. 50.
4. Use for dyeing only those lichens that are conspicuously abundant.
5. Leave nine-tenths of the lichens undisturbed at sites where you collect.
6. Do not purchase lichens and do not sell them to other dyers.
7. Never collect at parks, historic sites or protected areas.
8. Do not use lichen dyes for large textile projects that require more than 3 k (6.6 lb) of yarn.
9. Avoid using lichens to make unexceptional dye colours (e.g., beige).

10. Avoid using lichens at workshops where the leader lacks botanical expertise.
11. Avoid group collecting, and set a good example by your own collecting methods: see p. 51.
12. Self-educate in regard to conservation issues: habitat destruction (e.g., the building of roads associated with housing/cottage development and recreational land use) impacts on lichens—be it in Norway, New Mexico, or Nova Scotia.

Lichens and Dye Pigments

Lichens contain substances (depsides, depsidones) that are dye precursors. Sources that deal with this aspect include Brough 1984–88, Grierson et al. 1985, Richardson 1988, and Solberg. Biochemical structures of acids and dyes are in Casselman 1994b, Grierson et al. and Sandberg 1997. All lichens contain acids, so technically, any of the hundreds of genera commonly available can be used for dyeing. But some lichen acids are more effective as dye precursors than others. To avoid waste, it helps to know which lichens contain which substances (depending upon the lichens available: see above). A safe and simple test, the C test, can help you detect the presence of specific acids.

CHART 5a: DYE-PRODUCING SUBSTANCES (LICHEN ACIDS)

Acid	Type of dye	Reaction	Typical species
atranorin	BWM	K+ yellow	Hypogymnia physodes Platismatia glauca
erythrin	AM	C+ red	Roccella and Diploschistes spp.
fumarprotocetraric	AM BWM	P+ red*	Cetraria islandica
gyrophoric	AM	C+ red	Lasallia and Ochrolechia spp. all Umbilicaria spp. except U. cylindrica
lecanoric	AM	C+ red KC+ red	Parmelia fuliginosa P. glabratula Punctelia rudecta
lobaric	BWM	K+ yellow	Lobaria pulmonaria
parietin	POD	K+ purple	Xanthoria spp.
usnic	BWM	K+ yellow	Xanthoparmelia conspersa

*P = paraphenylenediamine: this reagent is carcinogenic; use only in a fully equipped lab, or better still, avoid it. Few women realize that "P" is one ingredient in ammonia-free hair dyes and henna.

Chemical Reagents (The C Test)

The C test (or C/K test) is used to identify lichen substances. Reagents (see Glossary) include C (calcium hypochlorite), which is household bleach; and K or KOH (potassium hydroxide), which is lye or drain cleaner (Chart 4, p. 43). The +/- sign means that a positive colour reaction (or a negative reaction, as in C-) occurs when the lichen is tested. Note: Your field guide will indicate whether the test is made to the lichen *thallus* or to the *medulla* (see Glossary).

Use a knife to scrape away a small spot on the upper cortex of a dry lichen; this exposes the white medulla. With a cotton swab or pipe cleaner, apply a drop of C to this white spot (or to the thallus; the field guide will say which). Lichens that react C+ red are suitable for AM dyes. K test: apply a drop of K to the thallus or medulla. Lichens that react K+ are suitable for BWM dyes. (Most C- lichens are also K+.)

Lecanoric acid is among those substances that cannot be detected without using two reagents, C and K. Your field guide will describe these species. To do the KC test: apply a drop of K, followed immediately by a drop of C, to the same spot on the lichen thallus or medulla.

How to Learn Lichen Identification

People will sometimes ask how I learned to identify lichens. Implicit in their question is the idea that it is difficult, but this is not the case. Sometimes I make the comparison to birding (p. 4), where patience and identification aids are helpful. A field guide is essential to learn how to correctly identify lichens by their botanical name, a detail which is not required for birds, but necessary when dealing with plants. Guides include useful diagrams and colour photographs that will help you to recognize lichens in their natural habitat. Field guides also include distribution maps, and they describe the relative abundance of particular species (Chart 5b, p. 52).

The only other equipment needed is a hand lens (also called a "loupe") and an old basket or container (avoid plastic bags). Wait for a foggy or damp day: wet lichens are soft and that's the best time to remove them. If you collect moist lichens on cemetery monuments, it is important to use a flexible blade, which will not scratch the stone; a rubber spatula also works well.

You can learn on your own or with a friend, but avoid group collecting the way that mushroom dyers do; for in spite of seasonal harvesting, fungi regrow every year. Another way to accelerate the learning curve is to join a nature club or society that sponsors field trips. Remember that public field trips are for *learning*; this is not the time to collect lichens for dyeing or to focus on that as your sole reason for attending. Visit herbaria (see Glossary) or find a mentor at a local university.

When you have learned five common species, take your field guide on a foray to the local cemetery. See if you can find *Xanthoria*. Your field guide will probably describe several species of this genus (Chart 3c, p. 31) and explain that *Xanthoria* varies in colour from bright orange (when the thallus is in full sun) to greenish-yellow (in the shade). The field guide will also describe the "rimmed apothecia" characteristic of *X. parietina* and give the chemistry: K+ purple (try this on a piece of the thallus—it's very dramatic). Now check the distribution map. Is *Xanthoria* common here? Notice the other lichens growing on the same stones. *Physcia* is a typical cemetery lichen whose whitish-grey thallus is very conspicuous when compared to orange *Xanthoria*. Greenish *Xanthoparmelia* spp. also occur on cemetery stones.

Remove an entire specimen of each species you think you can identify. Examine it with your hand lens: do your samples match those described in the field guide? At home, dry your specimens thoroughly by pressing them flat between several sheets of newspaper. (Weight them with books.) Keep changing the paper and make certain the specimens are entirely dry. Then place each lichen inside a folded paper packet; label it with the Latin name, collection site, date, and C and K test results; and file in a shoebox for your personal lichen herbarium.

Sometimes you will observe that lichens of the same species appear unalike. Lichens also change colour when wet (field guides generally state whether the lichen pictured was photographed wet or dry). Moreover, lichen chemistry is complex. Not all specimens will react as you predict: one umbilicate lichen is C- (*U. cylindrica*, Chart 5a, p. 48). The chemistry of *Evernia prunastri* is also unusual; when tested, this lichen often reacts C-, K- or KC- (Culberson). I have experimented with North American specimens of *E. prunastri* and found them not effective for dyeing by any method. This species is abundant on the West Coast and in northern Europe, where it is used both as an AM (Chart 3c, p. 31) and a BWM (Chart 3d, p. 34) dye. Geographic variation in lichen substances is one reason for this discrepancy.

"Found" Lichens

"Found" lichens are unattached to substrate, and they are found everywhere. City streets and lawns after winter storms are littered with twigs and branches covered with urban-tolerant species such as *Evernia mesomorpha*, *Hypogymnia physodes*, *Parmelia sulcata* and *Platismatia glauca*. Many species of *Usnea* fall to the forest floor; underfoot, they will inevitably be destroyed by recreational vehicles, human traffic or snow cover. Where there is active logging, woodlots are littered with *Lobaria pulmonaria*. (In a southern Alaska forest, I saw ditches full of *Lobaria*, lichens that would be snow-covered and thus ruined the following winter.) A considerable volume of lichen is wasted during orchard pruning; examples are *Flavoparmelia caperata*, *Parmelia sulcata* and *Physcia* spp. Fences, stone walls and coastal rocks are often covered so thickly with *Xanthoria* spp. that the lichens blow away.

When looking for lichens, ecology and geography are important factors: granite generally indicates the presence of umbilicate lichens. On a river in central Sweden, I once saw a phenomenal sight—as many as 200 boulders actually *in* a river were completely covered with *Lasallia pustulata*. This prodigality is also typical of parts of Canada and the USA. Norway has 12–15 species of *Umbilicaria*, but in England, umbilicates are nowhere near as abundant as other AM species (check UK sources in Charts 3c, p. 31, and 3d, p. 34).

Boulders and outcrops covered with *Lasallia* and *Umbilicaria* are a treasure trove. Lichens are soft when wet and tear easily. This is an advantage when collecting umbilicates, for you can remove pieces from the edge of large specimens (e.g., *U. mammulata*) without destroying the thallus or even removing it; if the umbilicus of the lichen remains attached, the lichens will continue to grow. Use this approach when you collect lichens still attached to substrate. You can also find enough pieces to make an AM vat by sifting through debris at the base of rocks. Learn to appreciate that large umbilicate lichens may be hundreds of years old. Respect these organisms as you would any other botanical specimen of mature years.

Look around and see what's plentiful. Use what nature provides, free for the taking. In the forest behind my house, *Evernia mesomorpha*, *Hypogymnia physodes* and *Plastimatia glauca* drop daily to the ground. This is my apparently endless supply, but instead of volume dyeing, my passion involves the lichens themselves, and researching their colourful history.

In ethical and environmental terms, it makes sense to mix lichens in a single dye bath: this puts less pressure on specific dye species and makes collecting easier, too. Combine lichens in the AM or BWM dye bath according to the type of dye acids they contain: see Chart 5a, p. 48.

1. Leave nine-tenths of the lichens at any site undisturbed.
2. Do not detach large lichens: remove only a portion so the thallus will continue to grow.
3. When there is a choice, use "found" (unattached) lichens rather than attached specimens.
4. Avoid group outings where collecting dye lichens is the goal.

5. Gather no more than you plan to use immediately. Yes, you can store lichens, but why hoard bags and bags of material better left in nature? Plan lichen projects with care. Make each lichen-dye bath a special event.

CHART 5b: INTERNATIONAL LICHEN FIELD GUIDES

Region	Author(s) and publication date	Comments
Australia	Filson 1986; Filson and Rogers 1979	checklist of continent and key to southern Australian species*
Britain and Ireland	Purves et al.	definitive, comprehensive key*
Canada	Brodo, Sharnoff and Sharnoff 2001	only lichen guide for all of North America; see Bibliography
Europe	Jahns et al. 1983	colour-illustrated field guide
Japan	Ikoma 1983	illustrated key and field guide
New Zealand	Martin and Child 1972	checklist, key*
North America	Brodo, Sharnoff and Sharnoff 2001	only lichen guide for all of North America; see Bibliography
North America	Hale 1979	popular classic: b/w photos, maps*
North America (northern)	Thompson 1984	key and guide; outstanding botanical illustrations and distribution maps*
North America (northwestern)	Vitt, Bovey and Marsh 1988	many photos of common lichens in popular regional field guide*
Norway	Krog et al. 1994	key and guide; b/w photos and maps*
Sweden	Moberg 1982	key and guide; colour photos*
Western hemisphere	Llano 1950	classic monograph on umbilicates, maps, b/w photos*

Symbols: "field guide" = an illustrated book for general reader; "key" = taxonomic study; "checklist" = non-illustrated list of species; * check local university libraries and second-hand booksellers.

Note: illustrated magazine articles about lichens (e.g., Sharnoff and Sharnoff 1997) are a good way to learn about their biology and ecology. To date, the only general study on lichens that includes their use in dyeing is Richardson 1975. Dye and medicinal information is also in Richardson 1988 and 1991.

Epilogue

There can be no positive future for a set of practices which are
. . . artificially kept alive out of a sense of duty or false tradition.

—Paul Greenhalgh, "The Progress of Captain Ludd"

Greenhalgh is right; a sense of false tradition plagues cultural practices too little known today to be evaluated on their own merits. Lichen dyeing is perhaps the prime example of this tendency. For in some places, lichen dyeing is kept artificially alive as a form of cultural re-enactment done to please tourists. Crottle generates money. People will buy crottle-dyed cloth (and pay more for it) if they are told that's what it is.

The Harris tweed industry appropriated crottle for marketing purposes (p. 17). Books on Scottish craft perpetuate the notion that lichen dyes are still in use in that trade. Examples include Carter and Rae's *Traditional Scottish Crafts* (Edinburgh, 1988) and J. MacKay's *Rural Crafts in Scotland* (London, 1976). Evidence is provided by the weaver/dyer who, when interviewed, draws attention to lichens displayed in the studio. Thus the interviewer equates proximity with practice.

Who has the experience to see the lack of veracity in a persuasive but artificial portrayal? Who knows how much crottle one can harvest and process in a season? How much it takes to dye yarn to weave 20 yards of tweed? How and where the best lichens grow? Among the cultural tourists now flocking to areas such as the Outer Hebrides are weavers, spinners and dyers who *do* know. And I realize that in order to perpetuate lichen dye research as a valid form of academic inquiry, we must first scrape away the "fakelore" that obscures the tradition.

The historiography of the subject is full of contradiction, paradox and deception. How did dyes that were once synonymous with rank and status become synonymous with rural poverty? Was the purple of Viking Dublin a northern orchil equivalent or a northern form of murex? Why is it that historians continue to describe orchil as a tradition that died after the fall of Rome when there is abundant evidence (see Furley and Hunt) to the contrary? What explains the discrepancy between the fortune and legacy of the Gordons and Lunds? And of these two families, why are the Lunds today less known than the bankrupt Scots?

We need to support not artificial histories of traditional practice, but inquiry into this rich narrative that reflects aspects of gender, ethnicity, culture, and ecology. We need to foster research that illuminates actual practice, past and present; shed light on the reconceptualization of dyeing as agriculture, education, science, and history; and, in my opinion, recognize the cultural value of analysis that accurately identifies the ethnicity, gender, and domestic labour status of the dye maker.

We have here a considerable task. One primary obstacle is attitude. For example, until recently, there has been no single document that analyses the dozens of vernacular lichen dye names within a socioeconomic and historical context. (My study, "A Lexicon of European AM and BWM Lichen Dyes," was published in 2000. See Diadick Casselman 2000b.) But the European textile journal to which it was first submitted was unable to find a sympathetic peer reviewer. The editor cited as one reason "the arcane nature of the subject which is today of little interest to textile scholars." Am I to believe that none of the 10,000 who have attended my lectures during the past 20 years are scholars? Or that my research in ten countries would be of no interest to any of that group? Perhaps a better question is how there can be a "positive future" in a subject where the very mythology that characterizes the field is matched in magnitude by professional skepticism, misapprehension and, apparently, misjudgement and mistrust?

What accounts for the willingness with which individual members of the British Lichen Society generously assist dye research—despite their collective view that lichen dyeing should generally be discouraged other than as a research subject? And what justifies national craft organizations—in the same country and at the same time—in putting obstacles in the way of identifying and locating their own craft pioneers (such as Eileen Bolton, among others; see Casselman 1992d–e)? What causes world-class libraries to dismiss the apparent loss of significant primary source material (pp. 19, 24) as "library leakage"?

Ethnicity and gender may be larger issues than we have recognized. What happens if, by illuminating the history of lichen dyeing, we cast doubt—as I have done—on the veracity of contemporary practice? What happens when the presumed ethnic origins of specific dyes are challenged? Is it unacceptable to revisit that history? And are results of such research less satisfactory and less acceptable when the reinterpretation comes not from *within,* but from without?

The ultimate irony here is that lichen-dye research has redirected attention toward an ethical matter of considerable urgency: the exploitation of lichens in central and southeast Europe, where prime harvesting regions are now war zones. Moxham is one of the few to mention the paradox of the expensive perfumes made from the fruits of that labour and the poverty of the lichen harvesters, who are often women. I have argued, in my 1999 thesis, that this ethical debate should take precedence over exaggerated concerns about craft dyeing. I also see a fundamental distinction between harvesting for commercial industry, and textile dyeing as an *occasional* and *individual* pursuit.

Nor has adequate attention been paid to gender-specific lichen uses. The recipe for an Andalusian menstrual tea made with lichens and wine (see Gonzáles-Tejero) is typical of pharmaceutical studies, in which folk medicine is now research. Such uses are of interest to scientists today in their efforts to understand the mysteries of lichen biology, ecology and morphology. Lichen dyes—made now, and in the past, primarily by women—are thus linked through time and space to larger human concerns in science, health and healing, and environmental awareness.

Greenhalgh also addresses the need to close what he calls the "unpleasant space between the arts and sciences." Lichen dye studies offer a remarkable opportunity to do just that. But "false traditions" are all we will have if we accept careless lichen dye research and writing. Like Greenhalgh, I prefer veracity and history; and instead of "a sense of duty," a sense of intellectual curiosity. And I would go further and suggest that the future of dyeing as a craft depends on analysis and scrutiny within an academic framework, where praxis is one component of history that is ever fluid over time. If practice changes—and it does—so must we accommodate culturally as we record it, describe it, and do it. To fail is to relegate craft to the margin of culture, while in the past it has been at the centre of human activity. Lichen dye studies can help prevent the erosion of craft as praxis, but only if we acknowledge what it is now—and what it can be in the future.

Photographs and Illustrations

The following books, articles, and monographs I have written contain illustrative material relevant to this text. The letters used (e.g., Casselman 1993e and 1993f) correspond to entries in the Bibliography, p. 67. Photocopies of articles are available. Send queries (including full title and year of publication) to the author at Cheverie, Nova Scotia, Canada B0N 1G0.

"COV" indicates a *colour* cover (or covers) of the magazine or journal that contains the article.

aeration or fermentation in AM vats	Casselman 1992c
alternative mordants	Casselman 1993c
AM-dyed skeins	Casselman 1978, 1980, 1986, 1993a, COV 1994b, 1996b, 1996c
AM-dyed fabrics	Casselman 1980, 1986, 1996b, 1996c
AM-dyed fleece	Casselman 1992c, COV 1992e
AM-dyed knitting	Casselman 1992c
AM dye vat	Casselman 1992c
BWM-dyed wools	Bolton 1991, Casselman 1993e
BWM lichens	Bolton 1991, Casselman COV 1992d, 1993f, 1994b
Cemetery lichens	Casselman 1991, 1992a
POD dyes	Casselman 1993e, 1996
POD lichens	Casselman 1991, 1992a, 1992c
G. Bærentsen photo	Casselman 1993e
E. Bolton photo	Casselman 1992d, 1992e

G. Sandberg photo

C/K test
Hand lens

Actinogyra muehlenbergii
Lasallia papulosa

Umbilicaria spp.

Lund house, Norway
Murex shells
Norse lichen dyes

Plictho
Westring 1805

Eco Dyes
Verdigris and alternative mordants

Casselman 1993e

Casselman 1992c
Casselman 1992c

Casselman 1980, 1986, 1993a
Bolton 1991, Casselman 1980, 1986, 1992c, 1992d, 1992e, 1993a, 1994b
Casselman 1978, 1979, 1980, 1992c, 1993a, 1994b

Casselman 1993e, 1996c
Casselman 1992a
Casselman 1993e, COV 1993f, COV 1994b, 1996c
Casselman 1994b, 1994c
Casselman 1990b, 1992c, COV Casselman 1994b

Casselman 1996a, 1996b, 1998a
Casselman 1996b, 1997, 1998a

Glossary

acids, lichen	*see* substances
adjective	dye that requires mordant; *see* substantive
aerate	to incorporate oxygen
AM	ammonia method; a vat process; *see* "fermentation"; originally "AFM" (see Brough 1984, 1988)
apothecia	cup-shaped discs on the upper cortex of the lichen that contain asci (spores)
binomial	system of naming plants and animals by genus and species
BWM	boiling water method; a direct dye process in which lichen pigments are extracted in water; term originated by S. Brough; *see* AM
C or C/K test	test using reagents that indicate which lichen substances (acids) are present
cortex	either surface (top: dorsal, or upper cortex; bottom: ventral, or lower cortex) of a lichen thallus
crocking	phenomenon that occurs when unbonded dye particles rub off or transfer to another substrate
cryptogams	plants that lack seeds and flowers (fungi, lichens, etc.)
fermentation	orcein production in AM vats; technically, decomposition or "putrefaction"
genus	a "family" group of similar plants (plural "genera")
herbarium	a collection or library of flora specimens kept for study purposes

hypobranchial	a gland or sac in certain species of molluscs; contains a toxic fluid
lichen	symbiotic biological entity composed of algal and fungal partners
lichenology	the science and study of lichens
macrolichen	large and conspicuous lichens (e.g., umbilicates)
medulla	layer of hyphae below the upper cortex and algal layer of a lichen thallus; in most lichens, the medulla is white
mordant	dye additive, often in the form of chemical salts, that affects results and improves fastness
murex	one name for mollusc dyes; other names include "Royal" and "Tyrian purple"
mycology	study of fungi, specifically mushrooms
niddy noddy	a wooden device held in the hand and used to wind skeins (illustrated in spinning books)
orcein	the substance to which orcinol is converted in AM dyes
orcinol	substance formed by the decomposition of certain lichen substances (depsides, depsidones)
orsallia	North American AM dye made from a combination of lichens; first named in 1993 (see Casselman 1993a)
POD	photo-oxidized blue lichen dyes made using *Xanthoria* spp.
reagent	substance used as an agent in a chemical process
resist	device used to prevent uniform dye penetration as a means to create a pattern
sp., spp.	sp.: species, singular; spp.: species, plural
substances	aromatic chemical compounds (acids and other substances) unique to lichens; dye precursors; historical and modern applications include cosmetics and dyes
substantive	dye that technically does not require a mordant (e.g., a lichen dye)
substrate	surface such as a rock or tree to which a lichen is attached

thallus   the entire lichen (plural "thalli")

TLC   thin-layer chromatography; a lab procedure used to identify pigments and other compounds

Tyrian Purple   *see* murex

umbilicate   any of several groups of macrolichens (including the genera *Lasallia* and *Umbilicaria*) that are attached to substrate by means of an umbilicus

vernacular   characteristic of a certain place, culture, or form of cultural expression

Acknowledgements

Agencies that supported my research the past few years include the Canada Council, the Chalmers Fund for Craft, the Helen Creighton Foundation, the Sheila Hugh Mackay Foundation, the Pasold Research Fund (UK), and the Department of Foreign Affairs and Trade (Ottawa). I wish to acknowledge the technical support from the Nova Scotia Museum, and I am especially grateful to the Nova Scotia Arts Council, which assisted me with my 1998 Australia research.

For dyed samples I wish to thank Reidun Almedal (Norway), Gunnvør Bærentsen (Færoe Islands), Gretchen Becker (VT), LeeAnn Bryant (Ontario), Armorel Carlyon (England), Cecilia Clements (PA), Glenna Dean (NM), Barbara Dowds (British Columbia), Ing Flint (Australia), Fred Gerber (TN), Su Grierson (Scotland), Elsa Grude (BC), Susan Hopkins (NJ), Thomas and Leslie Kilbride (Scotland), Gerd Mari Lye (Norway), Alicia Marr (Nova Scotia), Anne Marie Moroney (Ireland), Nel Ouderman (New Brunswick), Marjean Parks (BC), Ted Roubal (WA), Gösta Sandberg (Sweden), Kristie Sherrodd (Alaska), Ellen Stone (RI), Anita Dyer Swann (CA), Katrina Syme (Australia), June Upton (England), and Rose Wirtz (NJ). I also appreciate Eco Dye samples sent to me by students in four countries; this material is acknowledged in *Ethical and Ecological Dyes*.

Among the alumni of my annual seminar at the Humboldt Field Research Institute in Maine, thanks are due to Marian Allen, who greatly facilitated an Alaska research trip; Pauline Duke, whose idea to use lichens as mordants I stole; knitting author Marilyn van Keppel, who made murex; Sarah Killam and Kathy Cannon, who gave me special books; and Rose Wirtz, basket maker/dyer/rug designer extraordinaire who shares my passion for ethnic textile traditions. Humboldt (aka "Eagle Hill") director Jeorg-Henner Lotze and his mother, Ingrid, continue to support, at the Maine station, intellectual investigation into all living organisms, including those that yield dyestuffs of historical and cultural value. I am grateful for their helpfulness. Among other Humboldt alumni who deserve special thanks are Sara Kadolph and Laurann Gilbertson. It was at the

1998 class that we first conceived the plan to coordinate an international natural dye conference. Colour Congress 2002 will take place at Iowa State University, May 19–21, the result of our shared vision.

Among the Canadian arts and crafts pioneers whose friendship has made a considerable difference to me, I have the privilege to include Dorothy Burnham, Maberly, Ontario; Mary Sparling, Halifax; and former Canadian Craft Council President, Patricia Pollett McClelland, who, when I was her student 30 years ago, first brought Eileen Bolton's work to my attention. Dawn MacNutt loaned me her murex results and shared other natural-dye research. Chris Tyler, Department of Culture and Tourism, deserves thanks for bringing to my attention Peter Dormer's *The Culture of Craft* (see Epilogue). Chris also included my mixed-media work in a 1998 exhibition at the Art Gallery of Nova Scotia, an opportunity that allowed me to demonstrate lichen dye applications beyond fibre.

I am also grateful to Rita Adrosko, who peer-reviewed my first manuscript and later acquired one of my lichen-dyed textiles for the Smithsonian Institution; Jacqueline Ross, who was responsible for the McCord Museum (Montréal, Quebec) acquisition; Penelope Walton, for the Jorvik commission (York, UK); the late Gösta Sandberg (Nora, Sweden), for his interest in my research; and Jim Liles, who made it possible to develop a friendship with Fred Gerber. Australia fibre friends and colleagues who have assisted my work include TAFTA's Janet DeBoer and board member Peggy Buckingham; Katie Syme, Denmark SA; and "Violetta Tinctoria" of Mt. Pleasant, SA, who is felt maker and dyer Ing Flint. Nova Scotia colleagues who lent moral support include ethnologist Ruth Holmes Whitehead and women's scholar Sharon MacDonald.

David Richardson and Jack Laundon both encouraged me to make conservation a priority. This influence is reflected in my research as a 1999–2001 Gorsebrook Fellow at Saint Mary's University, Halifax, where Dr. Richardson, as Dean of Science, participated on my thesis committee. SMU graduate advisors Dr. John G. Reid and Dr. Colin Howell set an example of excellence, both as individuals and as scholars, that was as exhilarating as it was challenging. They helped me develop confidence in my interpretation of history, but I alone am responsible for errors and omissions in what I write. That the sum result has value is in no small part due as well to two other thesis advisors, G. Douglas Vaisey, SMU Collections Librarian, and clothing and textiles specialist Dr. Sara Kadolph, Iowa State University.

Translation has been generously provided, over many years, by a coterie of friends and colleagues: Reidun Almedal and Torstein Engelskjon (Norway); Karen Finch, OBE (Britain); Marianne Sandberg Lauzon and Brighetta Wallace Ferguson (Canada); Kay Larson (USA); and Marjatta Rautiala (Finland). All were more helpful than they realize.

Among the many librarians who assisted me, I am especially grateful to G. Douglas Vaisey of the Patrick Power Library at Saint Mary's University, for his diligence, and to interlibrary loan's Sandra Hamm. Other librarians who assisted me include my sister, Cynthia Tanner (BC Legislature), who over the years has located many obscure sources, not the least of which was an address for George Llano, a man who has since become a friend. Wendy Robertson (University of Iowa), also provided ancient and medieval sources to enrich this study. Among those who provided rare books, herbarium specimens, archival and other materials, are Brian Coppins (Royal Botanic Gardens, Edinburgh); Judy Davis (Mittigong, Australia); Karen Finch, OBE (London); Albert Henderson (Leeds); J.R. Laundon (London); D.H.S. Richardson (Halifax); Sharon MacDonald (Halifax); and Maureen Williams (Brewer Celtic Collection, Saint Francis Xavier University, Antigonish, NS).

Ted Casselman and George Llano, between them, are to blame for conspiring to gift me with the copy of Westring 1805 that I so cherish. The opportunity Ted and I had to spend time with George here in Nova Scotia remains a very happy memory.

Julia Bolton Holloway, who now lives in Italy, continues to inspire me with her medievalist's heart, eye and spirit.

My family (Ted, Tracy, and Tanya; and my mother, Pauline Diadick), have supported me in my indulgence for this work. That it has become my passion is due to their patience and encouragement to depart from the ordinary in life. I also appreciate the time spent by Tracy and Ted, who cooked, gardened, drove, and proofread so that this project could be completed concurrently with the writing of my thesis.

Lastly, the change in my name was one of the last gifts I gave my father, Fred Diadick. Occasionally it causes minor inconvenience (to librarians and editors, for example), but he was pleased by this small gesture. And since his recent death, I am certain it was the right way to honour him.

Annotated Bibliography

Note: Authors (and journals: see p. 23) change their names. Walton is both "Rogers" and "Walton Rogers"; I am K. L. Casselman, K. D. Casselman, and since 1997, K. Diadick Casselman. For non-English books and articles, see pp. 76–78. References in square brackets [ ] are to pages in *this* text.

SOURCES IN ENGLISH

Adrosko, R. 1971. *Natural Dyes & Home Dyeing*. Republication 1968 National Museum Bulletin 281; *Natural Dyes in the United States*. Dover Publications, Inc., New York. (Often confused with 1935 Department of Agriculture Bulletin # 230, *Home Dyeing with Natural Dyes* by Furry & Viemont, which this book includes.)

Aiken, M. 1970. Lichens as a dye source. *Craftsman/L'Artisan*, Vol. 3 (3), pp. 16–18. (This important Canadian source is undervalued; it was instrumental in the development of my work.)

Antúnez de Mayolo, K. 1989. Peruvian natural dye plants. *Economic Botany*, Vol. 43 (2) pp. 181–191.

Baker, J. T. 1975. Tyrian purple: an ancient dye, a modern problem. *Conchologists Newsletter*, No. 53 (June), pp. 428–443.

Bancroft, E. 1814. *The Philosophy of Permanent Colours*. Cadell & Davies, Philadelphia. (This is the 2nd London edition, published the following year in America). [See p. 20.]

Barber, E. J. W. 1999. *The Mummies of Ürümchi*. Norton, New York. 1991. *Prehistoric Textiles: The Development of Cloth in the Neolithic and Bronze Ages*. Princeton University Press, Princeton, N.J.

Bearfoot, W. 1975. *Mother Nature's Dyes and Fibres*. Oliver Publishers, Willits, Cal.

Bemiss, E. 1973. *The Dyer's Companion*. Dover Publications, Inc., New York (facsimile of 1815 edition; Foreword by Adrosko). [See p. 20].

Benson, A. 1966. *The America of 1750: Travels by Peter Kalm*. Vol. 1 & 2. Dover Publications, Inc., New York (see also Kerkkonen).

Blunt, W. and S. Raphael. 1979. *The Illustrated Herbal*. Thames & Hudson, New York.

Bolton, E. 1991. *Lichens for Vegetable Dyeing.* Robin & Russ Handweavers, McMinnville, Or. (Revised American 2nd ed., co-edited by J. Bolton Holloway and K. L. Casselman; it contains the story of how I found Eileen, and how Julia found me).

Born, W. 1937. Purpura shellfish. Purple in antiquity. *CIBA Review,* No. 4, pp. 106–127.

Brightman, F. H. and J. R. Laundon. 1985. *Alternatives to lichen dyes.* British Lichen Society, London. (A two-page pamphlet suggesting alternative dyestuffs.) [See Code of Ethics, p. 47 and Epilogue for a full discussion of the so-called "ethical debate."].

Brodo, I. M, S. D. Sharnoff & S. Sharnoff. 2001. *Field Guide to the Lichens of North America.* Yale University Press, New Haven, Conn. (Superbly illustrated new guide for all of the continent; see also Sharnoff & Sharnoff).

Bronson, J. & R. Bronson. 1977. *Early American Weaving and Dyeing (The Domestic Manufacturer's Assistant and Family Directory in the Arts of Weaving and Dyeing).* Dover Publications, Inc., New York. Reprint of 1817 revised edition. (Contains another of Adrosko's cogent introductions). [See p. 20.]

Brough, S. 1988. Navajo lichen dyes. *The Lichenologist,* Vol. 20 (3), pp. 279–290. (One of few serious studies to include aboriginal lichen dyes.)

———. 1984. Dye characteristics of British Columbia forest lichens. *Syesis* (British Columbia Provincial Museum),Vol. 17, pp. 81–94. Brough devised the terms "AFM" and "BWM". [See p. 48.]

Brunello, F. 1973. *The Art of Dyeing in the History of Mankind.* Trans. by B. Hickey. Phoenix Dye Works, Cleveland, Oh.

Burnham, H. & D. Burnham. 1972. *Keep Me Warm One Night.* University of Toronto Press, Toronto. (One of few historical studies to mention 19th century Canadian lichen dyes).

Campbell Thompson, R. 1934. An Assyrian Chemist's Vade-mecum. *Journal of the Royal Asiatic Society for Great Britain & Ireland,* pp. 771–785. (Contains a reference to *Xanthoria parietina* in ancient Assyria.)

Casselman, K. D. 1996a. Eco dyes. *The Woolcrafter* (Greymouth, New Zealand),Vol. 3 (1), p. 14.

———. 1996b. Natural dyes, naturally. *Journal of Weavers, Spinners & Dyers* (UK), Issue 177 (March), pp. 12–13.

———. 1996c. Norse lichen dyes. *Handwoven,* Vol. 17 (4), pp. 48–50. [Contains illustrations and maps relative to pp. 10–12.]

———. 1995. Dye pioneers (Fred Gerber, Winifred Shand). *Ontario Handweavers and Spinners Bulletin,* Vol. 38 (1), pp. 12–13.

Casselman, K. L. 1994a. Historical lichen dyes. *Norwegian Textile Newsletter,* Vol. 1 (1), pp. 1–8. (See also Diadick Casselman 1999b).

———. 1994b. Lichen dyes. *Maine Naturalist*, Vol. 2 (2), Pt. 1 (Ethics), pp. 61–70; Pt. 2 (Dyes), pp. 105–110.

———. 1994c. Lichen dyes: herb de l'orseille. *The Herbarist* (Kirtland, Ia.), No. 60, pp. 42–50.

———. 1993a. *Craft of the Dyer: Colour from Plants and Lichens*. 2nd edition, Dover Publications, Inc., New York. (Revised paperback edition of Casselman 1980).

———. 1993b. Environmental checklist for dyers. *Spin-Off*, Vol. 17 (2), pp. 96–98.

———. 1993c. Lichen dyes: ethics and environment. *The Wheel* (Ashburton, New Zealand), Issue No. 7, pp. 5–7.

———. 1993d. Reader's guide to lichen dyes. *Loomsong* (Atlantic Spinners & Handweavers, Halifax), Vol. 24 (4), pp. 16–19.

———. 1993e & f. Scandinavian dyes. *Ontario Handweavers & Spinners Bulletin*, Pt 1, Vol. 36 (2), pp. 10–13; Pt 2, Vol. 36 (3), pp. 5–7. (Contains photographs relevant to the Lund family and korkje; Færoese POD dyes, Sweden's G. Sandberg, Shetland & Fair Isle, etc.)

———. 1992a. Conservation, education, preservation: lichen dyes. *Nova Scotia Museum Occasional*, Vol. 13 (1), pp. 13–16.

———. 1992b. Ethical considerations of ancient and modern lichen dyes. Paper, International Association of Lichenologists Symposium #2, Båstad, Sweden, 36 pp.

———. 1992c. Lichen dye primer. *Spin-Off*,Vol. 16 (3), pp. 34–38. (The point of this article was to establish a base line for ethical craft use by providing basic AM/BWM procedures within an historical context, and correct Latin names of dye species.

———. 1992d. Searching for Eileen Bolton. *Journal Weavers, Spinners & Dyers* (UK), Issue 162, pp. 21–23. (One of two articles about Eileen Bolton; see below).

———. 1992e. Tribute: Eileen Bolton. *Heddle*, Vol. 8 (3), pp. 7–10.

———. 1991. Cemetery dyes. *Shuttle, Spindle & Dyepot*,Vol. 22 (3), pp. 32–33.

———. 1990a. 18th century dye manuals. *Ontario Handweavers and Spinners Bulletin*. Vol 33 (2), pp. 4–5.

———. 1990b. Lichens are important dyes. *Heddle*, Vol. 6 (4), pp. 6–9.

———. 1986. Colour magic from lichen dyes. *Shuttle, Spindle & Dyepot*, Vol. 17 (2), pp. 75–78.

———. 1980. *Craft of the Dyer: Colour from plants and lichens of the Northeast*. University of Toronto Press, Toronto.

———. 1979. Primeval dyes. *Harrowsmith*, No. 21, pp. 67–69.

———. 1978. Winter dyes from umbilicate lichens. *Shuttle, Spindle & Dyepot*,Vol. 9 (2), pp. 8–10.

68   Lichen Dyes: The New Source Book

Chambers, W. 1990. Arctic lichen dyes. In Buchanan, R.(ed.), *Dyes From Nature*. Brooklyn Botanic Garden Record, Vol. 46 (2), pp. 46–48.

Clow, A. & N. Clow. 1952. *The Chemical Revolution*. Batchworth, London. (An essential cudbear reference). [See pp. 10–12.]

Conley, E. 1957. *Vegetable Dyeing*. Penland, N.C.

Cooksey, C. 1997. Bibliography: lichen purple. *Dyes in History & Archaeology* (No. 15), pp. 103–110. Manchester meeting, published by Textile Research Associates, York, England; P. Walton Rogers, ed. (See also Dallon).

Crooks, W. 1874. *Dyeing and Calico Printing*. Longmans, Green & Co., London. (Information on industrial cudbear and orchil methods.)

Culberson, C. 1969. *Chemical and Botanical Guide to Lichen Products*. University of North Carolina Press, Chapel Hill, N.C.

Dallon, M. Orchil of Auvergne. 1996. *Dyes in History & Archaeology* (No. 15), pp. 97–102. (Dallon's lichen dyed skeins are featured on the cover.)

Davenport, E. 1972. *Your Yarn Dyeing*. Craft & Hobby Book Service, Pacific Grove, Cal.

Davidson, M. F. 1991. *The Dye-Pot*. Revised edition. Gatlinburg, Tenn.: Privately printed.

Dean, Jenny. 1999. *Wild Colour*. Mitchell Beazley, London; Watson-Guptill, New York. (K. Diadick Casselman, North American consulting editor.) [See p. 21.]

Densmore, F. 1974. *How Indians Use Wild Plants for Food, Medicine and Crafts*. Dover Publications, Inc., New York. (Published in 1928 as "Uses of Plants by Chippewa Indians", 44th Annual Report of the Bureau of American Ethnology.) [See p. 21.]

Diadick Casselman, K. 2001. *The Gorsebrook Papers*. Gorsebrook Institute, Nova Scotia Museum, Halifax, and Humboldt Institute, Steuben, Me. (Academic papers that address cultural, ecological, socio-economic, and feminist issues relevant to lichen dyes.

———. 2000a. A lexicon of European lichen dyes. *Dyes in History & Archaeology*, No. 18, Brussels Meeting (National Gallery, London).

———. 2000b. *Ethical and Ecological Dyes: A Work Book for the Natural Dyer*. Studio Vista Monograph No. 3, Cheverie, N.S.

———. 1999a. *An Annotated Bibliography of Lichen Dyes of Europe and North America* (Master's Thesis). Saint Mary's University, Halifax. (A survey of 500 primary and secondary sources AD 200–2000. Includes a comprehensive discussion of source material used for this text.)

———. 1999b. Norwegian korkje: myth and reality. *Norwegian Textile Letter*, Vol. 5 (2), pp. 1–7.

———. 1998a. Eco dyes: solutions for the future. *Textile Fibre Forum* (Australia), No. 51, pp. 28–29.

———. 1998b. Revival of interest in lichen dyes. *Wool Record* (UK), Vol. 157 (Issue No. 3648), pp. 57–59. (Cudbear, cork and crottle as the subject of research.)

———. 1997. Verdigris (Copper Acetate). *Shuttle, Spindle & Dyepot,* Vol. 28 (1), pp. 48–50. [See pp. 43–44.]

Edge, A. 1914. Some British Dye Lichens. *Journal of the Society of Dyers & Colourists* (UK), Vol. 30 (May), pp. 186–188.

———. 1915. The Colouring Matter of Tree Moss. *Journal of the Society of Dyers & Colourists* (UK),Vol. 31 (March), pp. 74–75.

Edmonds, J. 2000. *Tyrian or Imperial Purple Dye.* Historic Dye Series No. 7, Little Chalfont, Bucks, UK.

Edmondston, T. 1844. Paper on native dyes of the Shetland Islands. *Transactions of the Botanical Society of Edinburgh,* Vol. 1, pp. 123–126.

Encyclopedia Britannica. 1910. 11th edition, Vol 2. Cambridge University Press, Cambridge.

Esslinger, T. & R. Egan. 1995. A Fifth Checklist of the Lichen-forming, Lichenicolous and Allied Fungi of the Continental United States and Canada. *The Bryologist.* Vol 98 (4), pp. 467–549.

Filson, R. 1986. *Checklist of Australian Lichens.* 2nd edition. National Herbarium of Victoria, Melbourne.

Filson, R. & R. Rogers. 1979. *Lichens of South Australia.* South Australia Government, Adelaide.

Forbes, R. J. 1964. *Ancient Technology.* Vol. 4. Brill, Leiden.

Fraser, J. 1983. *Traditional Scottish Dyes.* Canongate, Edinburgh.

Furley, J. S. 1921. *Ancient Uses of the City of Winchester.* Oxford University Press, Oxford.

Furry, M. & B. Viemont. n.d. *Home Dyeing with Natural Dyes.* Thresh, Santa Rosa, Cal. (1935 republication Dept. of Agriculture Bull. #230, Washington; see Adrosko 1971.)

Galloway, D. 1985. *Flora of New Zealand Lichens.* New Zealand Government Printer, Wellington.

Gardner, W. M. 1896. Wool dyeing. Part 2. *Posselt's Textile Library,*Vol. VIII. Posselt Publisher, Philadelphia. pp. 37–70. (Fred Gerber sent me a copy of this very useful item on industrial orchil.)

Gerber, F. & W. Gerber. 1973. Dye plants of the deep south. In Weigle, P. (ed.), *Natural Plant Dyeing.* Brooklyn Botanic Garden Record, Vol. 29 (2), pp. 17–22.

———. 1969. Dyeing with lichens. *Handweaver & Craftsman,* Vol. 20 (2), p. 13ff. (Credit for "all that we know" is given in this article to Eileen Bolton's book.)

Gerhard, P. 1964. Shellfish dye in America. Sobretiro del XXXV Congresso Internacional de Americanistas (Mexico 1962), Actas y Memorias #3, pp. 177–191.

Gilbertson, L. 1998. Norwegian natural dyestuffs. *Norwegian Textile Letter*, Vol. 4 (2), pp. 9–11.

Gilbertson, L. & C. Colburn. 1997. *Handweaving in the Norwegian Tradition*. Vesterheim Norwegian American Museum, Decorah, Ia. (One of few contemporary exhibitions to link lichen dyes to immigrant clothing traditions in the American midwest).

González-Tejero, M. et al. 1995. Three lichens used in popular medicine in eastern Andalucia (Spain). *Economic Botany* 49 (1), pp. 96–98.

Goodwin, J. 1982. *A Dyer's Manual*. Pelham Books, London. (Author is a woad specialist octogenarian, and still active as a scholar.)

Gordon, C. 1791. *Memorial of Dr. Cuthbert Gordon relative to the discovery and use of cudbear, etc.* London. (A1786 petition to House of Commons.)

Gordon, F. 1980. Dyeing with *Sticta coronata*. Roseburg, Or. (Self-published booklet that contains more interesting and useful information than most. See also Merrill & Haight).

Goward, T. 1994. *The Lichens of British Columbia: Illustrated Keys*. Pt 1: Foliose and Squamulose Species. Report Series #8, Ministry of Forestry Research Program, Victoria, B.C. (Pt. 2: 1999.)

Grae, I. 1974. *Nature's Colours*. Macmillan Publishing, New York.

Greenhalgh, P. 1997. The progress of Captain Ludd. In P. Dormer (ed.), *The Culture of Craft*. Manchester University Press, Manchester, pp. 104–115. [See Epilogue, pp. 54–55.]

Grierson, S. 1989. *Dyeing and Dyestuffs*. Shire Publications, Aylesbury, Bucks. (Contains photograph of the "missing" Lindsay). [p. 24.]

———. 1986. *The Colour Cauldron*. Perth, Scotland. (When available, this was the only dye book in the Interweave catalog that contained *accurate* information on lichen dyes. Originally self-published, the later Interweave edition was offered at a bargain price. A fine book of careful research. (Compare Hoad 1987.)

———. 1984. Vegetable dyes of Scotland. *Journal of the Society of Dyers & Colourists*, Vol. 100 (July/August), pp. 209–211. (Grierson's articles are little-known; they deserve more attention than they generally receive.)

Grierson, S., D. G. Duff and R. S. Sinclair. 1985. The colour and fastness of natural dyes of the Scottish highlands. *Journal of the Society of Dyers & Colourists*, Vol. 101 (July/August), pp. 220–227.

Hadingham, E. 1994. The mummies of Xinjiang. *Discover*, Vol. 15 (4), April, pp. 68–77. (This little-known article contains better quality photographs of the garments of the Ürümchi mummies than does Barber 1999.)

Hale, M. E., Jr. 1979. *How to Know the Lichens*. Wm. C. Brown, Dubuque, Ia. (Long out of print, this beloved classic has been available as recently as 1998 from Robin & Russ, McMinnville, Or. It's worth a try to check with them.)

Hale, M. E., Jr. and M. Cole. 1988. *Lichens of California*. University of California Press, Berkeley.

Henderson, A. 1984–1985. Industrial manufacture of lichen dyestuffs. *British Lichen Society Bulletin* No. 55 (Winter 1984), pp. 19–21; No. 56 (Summer 1985), pp. 22–24; No. 57 (Winter 1985), pp. 12–14. See also Barbara Benfield's subsequent article in No. 58 (Summer 1986), pp. 18–20.

Hewitt, M. 1973. A substitute for a traditional dyestuff (cudbear). In P. Weigle (ed.) *Natural Plant Dyeing*. Brooklyn Botanic Garden Record,Vol. 29 (2), pp. 37–39.

Hoad, J. 1987. *This is Donegal Tweed*. Privately printed, Ireland. (Another self-published study which proves that well-researched, carefully edited books find a market. As valuable a work as Grierson's.)

Hofmann, R. 1997. The Bühler collection of Indonesian dye plants. *Dyes in History & Archaeology* (No. 15), pp. 3–26.

Hunt, Tony. 1995. Early Anglo-Norman Receipts for Colours. *Journal of the Warburg & Courtauld Institutes*, Vol. 58, pp. 203–209. (An important analysis of 12th century folios at the British Library; includes cork.)

Ikoma, Y. 1983. *Macrolichens of Japan and Adjacent Regions*. Tottori, Japan. (English translation).

Isham, J. *Isham's Observations and Notes 1743–1749*. The Champlain Society, Toronto, for the Hudson Bay Record: Series 12, 1949.

Jahns, H. 1983. *Collins Guide to the Ferns, Mosses and Lichens of Britain and North Central Europe*. Collins, London.

Jørgensen, L. and P. Walton. 1986. Dyes and fleece types in prehistoric textiles from Scandinavia and Germany. *Journal of Danish Archaeology*, Vol. 5, pp. 177–188.

Kavasch, E. B. 1979. *Native Harvests: Recipes and Botanicals of the American Indian*. Random House, New York. At a monastery in rural Connecticut, this author introduced me to the concept of "salvage botany."

Kerkkonen, M. 1959. *Peter Kalm's North American Journey*. Finnish Historical Society, Helsinki. (One of several English translations.)

Kok, A. 1966. A short history of orchil dyes. *The Lichenologist*, Vol. 3 (2), pp. 248–272. (Adefinitive reference: see also Perkins).

Krochmal, A. and C. Krochmal. 1974. *Complete Illustrated Book of Dyes From Natural Sources*. Doubleday, New York.

Laundon, J. R. 1986. *Lichens*. Shire Publications, Aylesbury, Bucks. (See also Brightman & Laundon.)

Leechman, D. 1932. Aboriginal Paints and Dyes in Canada. *Transactions of the Royal Society of Canada,* Section II, pp. 37–42. (Lichen dyes are not included in Leechman's better known *Vegetable Dyes from North American Plants.*)

Lewis, D. 1981. Dyeing with *Cetraria canadensis.* In A. Bliss (ed.), *A Handbook of Dyes from Natural Materials.* Charles Scribner's Sons, New York. (Also includes dyes by others, e.g. Padgham.)

Liles, J. 1990. *The Art and Craft of Natural Dyeing.* University of Tennessee Press, Knoxville.

Lindsay, W. L. 1856. *A Popular History of British Lichens.* Lovell and Reeve, London. (A beautiful book full of considerable detail on lichen dyes and their trade.) [See p. 24.]

———. 1854. Experimental researches on the tinctorial properties of lichens. *Edinburgh New Philosophical Journal,* No. 42, pp. 228–250; and *The Phytologist,* 1853, Vol. 4 & 5, pp. 867–872, 901–909, 998–1003, 1068ff. (Lindsay's articles were republished in several versions: see Lindsay 1856, p. 88, for his *own* list of these often misdated articles.)

Linnaeus, C. 1811. *Flora Lapponica.* J. E. Smith, London. Translation of the Latin original of 1737.

Llano, G. A. 1951. Economic uses of lichens. *Smithsonian Institution Annual Report 1950,* Washington, pp. 385–421; short version: see *Economic Botany,*Vol. 2 (1), 1948, pp. 15–45.

———. 1950. *Monograph of the Lichen Family Umbilicariaceae in the Western Hemisphere.* Navexos, pp. 1–281. Office of Naval Research, Department of the Navy, Washington. (A technical lichenological treatise of considerable value. The Nova Scotia Museum, Harvard's Farlow Reference Library and Lichen Herbarium have copies, as do I myself.) [See Acknowledgements, pp. 61–63.]

———. 1944. Lichens—their biological and economic significance. *The Botanical Review,* Vol. 10 (1), pp. 1–65. (Dr. Llano was then Dr. "Perez-Llano": see name note p. 65.)

Maclagan, R. C. 1898. On highland dyeing and colouring of native-made tartans. *Transactions of the Royal Scottish Society of Arts,* Vol. 14, pp. 386–410. (Few who mention this item have actually *seen* it: Grierson 1986 includes it but gives no page numbers. Fraser misspells the author's name.)

Mairet, E. *Vegetable Dyes.* 1952. Faber & Faber, London. (Next to Bolton, this is perhaps the most popular dye book of all time. There are at least 15 printings in two or three editions. The 1916 original edition includes Mairet's preface in which she impugns "hideous aniline dyes," a section unfortunately expunged from subsequent editions. The 1916 edition, on handmade paper, is a collector's item.)

Martin, W. & J. Child. 1972. *Lichens of New Zealand.* Reed, Wellington.

McClintock, H. 1950. *Old Irish and Highland Dress*. Dundalgan Press, Dundalk, Ireland. (See also Maclagan and O'Curry.)

McGrath, J. W. 1977. *Dyes from Plants and Lichens*. Van Nostrand Reinhold, Toronto.

McGuffin, N. 1986. *Spectrum: Dye Plants of Ontario*. Concord, Ontario.

McRae, B. A. 1993. *Colors From Nature: Growing, Collecting and Using Natural Dyes*. Storey, Pownal, Vt. (Valuable for general plant dye information, especially how to dye non-fibrous materials).

Merrill, R. & B. Haight. 1975. *Barbara an' Me: On Lichening & Learning*. Olympia, Wash. (A dreadful title camouflages what is valuable in this manual: low lichen-to-fibre ratios, clear instructions, and actual samples of the lichens used.) [I value my copy given to me by Humboldt alumnus Sarah Killam of Tennessee.]

Milner, A. 1992. *Ashford Book of Dyeing*. B. Williams Books, Wellington, New Zealand. (Brief but comprehensive section on New Zealand lichens.)

Mitchell, L. 1978. *Irish Spinning, Dyeing and Weaving*. Dundalgan Press, Dundalk, Ireland.

————. 1964. Recipes from Eire. In E. McD. Schetky (ed.), *Dye Plants and Dyeing*. Brooklyn Botanic Garden, Vol. 20 (3).

Moodie, S. 1962. *Roughing it in the Bush*. McClelland & Stewart, Toronto.

Moxham, T. 1986. The commercial exploitation of lichens. *Progress in Essential Oil Research*. E. Brunke (ed.). Walter de Gruyter, Berlin, pp. 491–503.

Mustard, F. 1977. *Dyeing the Natural Way*. Matteson, Ill.

Muthesius, A. 1993. The Byzantine silk industry: Lopez and beyond. *Journal of Mediaeval History*, Vol. 19, pp. 1–67. (A fascinating study in which the author revisits the Justinian Code and discovers that the "purple dyer" was not always a male worker.)

O'Curry, E. 1873. *Customs and Manners of the Ancient Irish*. Vol. 1 & 2. Williams & Norgate, London. (An Irish humanities classic which is controversial because, in spite of a rich narrative, it is said to be virtually impossible to trace the author's original Gaelic sources. Whether the lichen dye lore here is accurate or not, it is certainly abundant, and particularly detailed.)

Padgham, T. (See Lewis, in Bliss 1980).

Perkins, P. 1986. Ecology, beauty, profits: trade in lichen-based dyestuffs through Western history. *Journal of the Society Dyers & Colourists*,Vol. 102 (July / August), pp. 221–227. (An essential reference.)

Pliny the Elder. 1967. *Natural History III*, Books VIII–XI (70 AD). Harvard University Press, Cambridge, Mass.

Pocius, G. 1979. Textile traditions in eastern Newfoundland. Paper #29,

Canada Centre for Folk Culture Studies, National Museums, Ottawa. (One of few references to lichen dyes in Newfoundland.)

Pritchard, F. 1984. Late Saxon textiles from the city of London. *Mediaeval Archaeology*, No. 28, pp. 46–76.

Purvis, O. W. et al. 1992. *The Lichen Flora of Great Britain and Ireland*. British Lichen Society and Natural History Museum, London. [A better choice for the novice is Laundon 1986, or Jahns; see p. 52.]

Rambo Walker, Sandra. 1981. *Country Cloth to Coverlets*. Keystone Books, Lewisburg, Pa. (Aside from the Burnhams, and Gilbertson & Colburn, there are few references to lichen dyes in books on immigrant/settler textile traditions in North America; see also Pocius).

Richardson, D. H. S. 1991. Lichens and man. In D. Hawksworth (ed.), *Frontiers in Mycology*, 4th Congress 1990, C.A.B. International, pp. 187–210.

———. 1988. Medicinal and other economic aspects of lichens. In M. Galun (ed.), *CRC Handbook of Lichenology*, Vol. 3. CRC Press, Boca Raton, Fla., pp. 93–108.

———. 1975. *The Vanishing Lichens: Their History, Biology and Importance*. David and Charles, Newton Abbot, Devon. (Long out of print, this classic includes a photo of the most famous crottle dyer, whom I discuss at length in Diadick Casselman 1999a. [See Epilogue, pp. 53–55.] Dr. Richardson instructs a lichen class annually at the Humboldt Institute, Steuben, Maine.

Robertson, S. 1973. *Dyes From Plants*. Van Nostrand Reinhold, New York. (An older but useful classic.)

Robinson, J. Tyrian purple. *Sea Frontiers*, Vol. 17 (12), pp. 77–82.

Rosetti, G. 1969. *Plictho de l'arte de Tentori*. Translation and facsimile of 1548 edition by S. Edelstein & H. Borghety, MIT Press, Cambridge, Mass. [See p. 9.]

Roubal, T. 1996. Dyes from nature: coast lichens. *Oregon Coast*, Vol. 15 (6), pp. 48–50.

Rutt, R. 1990. *History of Knitting*. Batsford, London.

Rutty, J. 1990. *Indigenous Vegetables Useful in Dying* [sic]. D. Hill, (ed.). Facsimile chapter in 1772 *Natural History in the County of Dublin*. Dept. of Continuing Education, University of Bristol, UK.

Ryan, H. & W. O'Riordan. 1917. Tinctorial constituents of some lichens used as dyes in Ireland. *Royal Institute of Arts Proceedings*,Vol. 33. Sect. B, pp. 91–105.

Samuel, C. 1987. *The Raven's Tail*. University of British Columbia Press, Vancouver.

Sandberg, G. 1997. *The Red Dyes: Cochineal, Madder and Murex Purple*. Lark, Asheville, N.C. (See Diadick Casselman 1999a for a discussion of the circumstances surrounding the English translation of this book. Contains a section on dye chemistry by Sisefsky.)

Shand, W. *The Isles Are My Delight: A Tweed Trotter in the Outer Hebrides.* Privately published, Edinburgh. (The author was in life far more remarkable than this book reveals, visiting the Crimea past the age of 90; and singing a church solo days before she died. I treasure our 1985 and 1992 interviews during which she described swimming nude on beaches in the Hebrides.) [See Casselman 1995.]

Sharnoff, S. D. & S. Sharnoff. 1992. Lichens. *Equinox*, No. 65 (Sept /Oct), pp. 54–61. (See also Brodo et al; & *National Geographic*, Vol. 191 (2), February 1997, pp. 60–71.)

Simmons, J. 1985. *Shetland Dye Book.* Shetland Times, Lerwick, Shetland, Scotland.

Solberg, Y. 1956. Dyeing of wool with lichens and lichen substances. *Act Chemica Scandia*, Vol. 10, pp. 1116–1123. (A classic technical reference.)

Stenhouse, J. 1867. Notes on some varieties of orchella weed and products. *Chemical Society Journal*, Vol. 5, pp. 221–227.

Sverdrup, S. 1964. Dyes in Norway. In E. McD. Schetky (ed.), *Dye Plants and Dyeing.* Brooklyn Botanic Garden Record, Vol. 20 (3).

Taylor, G. 1990. Ancient textile dyes. *Chemistry in Britain.* December, pp. 1155-1158.

Taylor, G. & P. Walton. 1983. Lichen purples. In H. Dalrymple, (ed.), *Dyes on Historical & Archaeological Textiles* (8). National Museums of Scotland, Edinburgh, pp. 14–20. [See p. 22.]

Thomson, J. 1984. *American Arctic Lichens: The Macrolichens.* Irvington-on-Hudson, N.Y. (An outstanding reference.)

Thurston, V. 1970. *Use of Vegetable Dyes.* Dryad, Leicester, UK.

Turner, N. 1977. Economic importance of black tree lichen *Bryoria fremontii. Economic Botany*, Vol. 31, pp. 461–470.

Upton, J. 1990. Blue dyes from *Xanthoria* lichen. In R. Buchanan (ed.), *Dyes From Nature*, Brooklyn Botanic Garden Record, Vol. 46 (2), pp. 49–50.

Ure, A. 1824. *Elements of the Art of Dyeing.* Vol 2. Limpkin & Marshall, London. (English translation of C. & A. Berthold's 2nd French edition. Contains a noteworthy reference to Kalm and a red dye made from *Umbilicaria*, in Chapter 8.) [Compare Kalm's Pennsylvania dye, p. 20.]

Urquhart, J. 1993. *Away.* McClelland & Stewart, Toronto.

Van Stralen, T. 1993. *Indigo, Madder & Marigold.* Interweave Press, Loveland, Colorado.

Vitt, D., J. Marsh & R. Bovey. 1988. *Mosses, Lichens & Ferns of Northwest North America.* University of Washington Press, Seattle; Lone Pine, Edmonton, Alta.

Walton, P. 1989a. Dyes of the Viking Age. In P. Walton, (ed.) *Dyes in History and Archaeology*, No. 7, pp. 14–20. [See Taylor & Walton, p. 23.]

———. 1989b. *Textiles (cordage, etc.) from Coppergate*. Archaeology of York Series, Vol. 17 (5), pp. 283–454. (As the page numbers indicate, this is not an article but one book in a series.)

———. 1988. Dyes and wools in Iron Age textiles from Norway and Denmark. *Journal of Danish Archaeology,* Vol. 7, pp. 144–158. (This item is in English).

———. 1986. Dyes in early Scandinavian textiles. *Dyes on Historical and Archaeological Textiles* (5), pp. 38–43.

Walton, P. & G. Taylor. 1991. Characteristics of dyes in textiles from excavations. *Chromatography and Analysis*, Vol. 17, pp. 5–7.

Walton Rogers, P. 1993. Dyes and wool from Narsaq, Greenland. In Veboek, C. (ed.), Narsaq—A Norse Farm. Meddelelser om Grønland, *Man and Society*, Vol. 18, pp. 55–58. (13th-century purple lichen dyes of "exceptional depth" are described in this important paper.)

Weigle, P. 1974. *Ancient Dyes for Modern Weavers*. Watson-Guptill, New York.

Wickens, H. 1990. *Natural Dyes*. Batsford, London. (Brief but accurate lichen dye recipes.)

Windt, H. n.d. *Lichen dyes*. Privately printed. (A unique booklet once available from the author.)

Woodward, C. 1949. Vernacular names for *Roccella*. *Bulletin of the Torrey Botanical Club*, Vol. 76 (4), pp. 203–207. (An outstanding reference.)

Yacopino, P. 1973. A practical approach to the use of lichens. In P. Weigle, (ed.), *Natural Plant Dyeing*. Brooklyn Botanic Garden Record, Vol. 29 (2), pp. 29–32. (In all of the BBG dye books, this is one of the finest articles.)

Yeadon, D. 1990. Amid the crofters & weavers of tweed; Scotland's Outer Hebrides. *Washington Post* (Travel Section, Sunday, Aug. 26.). A romantic interpretation of Hebridean dyeing. [See Epilogue.]

SOURCES IN FOREIGN LANGUAGES

Bächi-Nussbaumer, E. 1980. *So Färbt man mit Pflanzen* (*Making Dyes with Plants*). Haupt, Bern and Stuttgart.

Bærentsen, G. 1987. *Liting vid Skonum* (*Dyeing with Lichens*). Privately printed, Tórshavn, Færoe Islands (Denmark). [See p. 46; colour photograph of the author with KDC in Casselman 1993e and f.]

Beriau, O. 1933. *La Teinturerie Domestique* (*Home Dyeing*). Ministrie de l'Agriculture, Quebec.

Berthollet, C. (See Ure for English translation).

Bremnes, G. 1979. Om fargebruk i "Døvle-teppet" (On the use of dyes in the "Døvle Coverlet"). *Utgitt av Vestfold Historielag, Vestfoldminne.* (English summary). [See Diadick Casselman 1999b for a discussion of Lunde's legacy.]

Christensen, H. 1935. *Lærebok i Farvning med Planter (Handbook of Dyeing with Plants)*. J. W. Cappelens, Oslo. (Includes lichen dyes in this later edition of the 1908 original.)

Dahl, E. and H. Krog. 1994. *Lavflora (Lichen Flora)* [of Norway]. Universitetsforlaget, Oslo. (A recent imprint of an earlier edition, this contains excellent photographs of Norway's many umbilicate species. [See p. 51 and Chart 5b, p. 52.]

Dambourney, L. 1794. *Histoire des Plantes qui Servant à la Teinture (A History of Plants Used for Dyeing)*. Paris. (A portion of this classic is reprinted in Adrosko 1971.)

Goubitz, N. 1973. *Verven met Plantaardige Stoffen (Dyeing with Useful Plants)*. Chanticleer, de Bilt, Netherlands. (*Cetraria icelandica* recipe).

Hoffmann, G. F. 1787. Commentatio de Vario Lichenum Usu (On the various uses of lichens). *Academie Science Belle Lettres Arts 3*, Lyon. (This is the Latin original with actual dyed samples as described in Llano 1951. [See p. 19.] Amoreaux, Hoffmann & Willemet 1787contains roughly the same information, but it is written in French. I have seen the latter and it lacks the actual dyed samples.)

Høiland, K. 1983. Laven korkje, *Ochrolechia tartarea* som fargeprodusent (Lichen korkje). *Blyttia,* Vol. 41, p. 17–21. (English abstract, photos.) [A letter from the author of this article motivated me find the Lista museum in 1992, and Samuel Watnee. See p. 8].

Konturri, H. 1947. *Luonnonväreillä Värjäämisestä (Dyeing with Natural Colours)*. (6th edition). Pellervo-Seura, Helsinki.

Lunde, D. 1976. Rød tråd: drakt og tekstil (Red thread [yarn] in dress and textiles). *Årbok 1972–75.* Kunstindustrimuseet, Oslo. (A contemporary translation shows that Lunde misunderstood the korkje process to such an extent that it was virtually impossible for her to succeed [Diadick Casselman 1999b]. Yet Lunde's paper is cited endlessly by experts who may not realize that the problem is *not the dye,* but the writer's misunderstanding of the entire dye process.)

Lye, G. M. & K. Arnstein Lye. 1981. Farging med lav (Dyeing with lichens). Sœrtrykk Väre Nyttevekster 1974/1975 (1), pp. 1–21.

Moberg, R. 1982. *Lavar: En Falthandbok (Lichens: a handbook)*. Interpublishing, Stockholm. (This book contains a photograph of Lindsay's sample book, as does Grierson 1989.)

Papyrus Graecus Holmiensis. 1913. Facsimile edition. Uppsala & Leipzig. (Swedish translation by O. Lagercrantz.)

Ploss, E. 1962. *Ein Buch von Alten Farben (A Book on Natural Dyes)*. Impuls,

Heidelberg.

Sandberg, G. 1994. *Purpur, Koschenill, Krapp: En Bok om Röda textilier* (*Purple, Cochineal and Lac: A Book on Red Textiles*). [Murex; contains entry on biochemical structures of red dyes by J. Sisefsky.]

Sandberg, G . & J. Sisefsky. 1980. *Växt Färgning.* (*Natural Dyeing*). Norstedt & Söners, Stockholm. (There are several earlier editions.)

Sauvé, P. 1977. *La Teinture Naturelle au Québec* (*The Natural Dyes of Quebec*). Les Éditions de l'Aurore, Montréal.

Svabo, J. C. 1782. *Indberetninger fra en Reise i Færøerne* (*A Winter Spent on the Færoes* 1781–1782). Copenhagen.

Teramura, Y. 1984. *Natural Dyes.* (In Japanese.) Atsushi Onuma, Tokyo. (Contains a photograph of indigo-dyed cotton overdyed with orchil.)

Westring, J. P. 1805. *Svenska Lafvarnas Färghistoria* (*The History of the use of Swedish Lichens in Dyeing*). Delén, Stockholm. This "book" is actually a series of pamphlets published between 1805 and 1809. [See p. 24 and Acknowledgements].

———. 1792. Sur la propriété tinctoriales des lichens. *Annales Chimie*, Vol. 15, pp. 267–297; see also 1793: Vol. 17, pp. 67–83.

———. 1791. Experiments on the dyeing properties of Scandinavian lichens. *Transactions of the Academy of Stockholm*, Vol. 12, pp. 113–138. (Kok includes these articles.)

Wold, S. & E. Nielsen (eds.). 1752. *Dorte Margete Rosenberg's Farvebog* (*Dorte Margete Rosenberg's Colour Book*). Facsimile edition, 1984. Blávandshuk Museum, Jutland, Denmark.

General Index

Name, Language, and Place Index

A CATALOG OF SELECTED
DOVER BOOKS
IN ALL FIELDS OF INTEREST

A CATALOG OF SELECTED DOVER
BOOKS IN ALL FIELDS OF INTEREST

CONCERNING THE SPIRITUAL IN ART, Wassily Kandinsky. Pioneering work by father of abstract art. Thoughts on color theory, nature of art. Analysis of earlier masters. 12 illustrations. 80pp. of text. 5⅜ x 8½.　　　23411-8 Pa. $4.95

ANIMALS: 1,419 Copyright-Free Illustrations of Mammals, Birds, Fish, Insects, etc., Jim Harter (ed.). Clear wood engravings present, in extremely lifelike poses, over 1,000 species of animals. One of the most extensive pictorial sourcebooks of its kind. Captions. Index. 284pp. 9 x 12.　　　23766-4 Pa. $14.95

CELTIC ART: The Methods of Construction, George Bain. Simple geometric techniques for making Celtic interlacements, spirals, Kells-type initials, animals, humans, etc. Over 500 illustrations. 160pp. 9 x 12. (Available in U.S. only.)　　　22923-8 Pa. $9.95

AN ATLAS OF ANATOMY FOR ARTISTS, Fritz Schider. Most thorough reference work on art anatomy in the world. Hundreds of illustrations, including selections from works by Vesalius, Leonardo, Goya, Ingres, Michelangelo, others. 593 illustrations. 192pp. 7⅛ x 10¼.　　　20241-0 Pa. $9.95

CELTIC HAND STROKE-BY-STROKE (Irish Half-Uncial from "The Book of Kells"): An Arthur Baker Calligraphy Manual, Arthur Baker. Complete guide to creating each letter of the alphabet in distinctive Celtic manner. Covers hand position, strokes, pens, inks, paper, more. Illustrated. 48pp. 8¼ x 11.　　　24336-2 Pa. $3.95

EASY ORIGAMI, John Montroll. Charming collection of 32 projects (hat, cup, pelican, piano, swan, many more) specially designed for the novice origami hobbyist. Clearly illustrated easy-to-follow instructions insure that even beginning papercrafters will achieve successful results. 48pp. 8¼ x 11.　　　27298-2 Pa. $3.50

THE COMPLETE BOOK OF BIRDHOUSE CONSTRUCTION FOR WOODWORKERS, Scott D. Campbell. Detailed instructions, illustrations, tables. Also data on bird habitat and instinct patterns. Bibliography. 3 tables. 63 illustrations in 15 figures. 48pp. 5¼ x 8½.　　　24407-5 Pa. $2.50

BLOOMINGDALE'S ILLUSTRATED 1886 CATALOG: Fashions, Dry Goods and Housewares, Bloomingdale Brothers. Famed merchants' extremely rare catalog depicting about 1,700 products: clothing, housewares, firearms, dry goods, jewelry, more. Invaluable for dating, identifying vintage items. Also, copyright-free graphics for artists, designers. Co-published with Henry Ford Museum & Greenfield Village. 160pp. 8¼ x 11.　　　25780-0 Pa. $12.95

HISTORIC COSTUME IN PICTURES, Braun & Schneider. Over 1,450 costumed figures in clearly detailed engravings–from dawn of civilization to end of 19th century. Captions. Many folk costumes. 256pp. 8⅜ x 11¾.　　　23150-X Pa. $12.95

THE INFLUENCE OF SEA POWER UPON HISTORY, 1660–1783, A. T. Mahan. Influential classic of naval history and tactics still used as text in war colleges. First paperback edition. 4 maps. 24 battle plans. 640pp. 5⅜ x 8½. 25509-3 Pa. $14.95

THE STORY OF THE TITANIC AS TOLD BY ITS SURVIVORS, Jack Winocour (ed.). What it was really like. Panic, despair, shocking inefficiency, and a little heroism. More thrilling than any fictional account. 26 illustrations. 320pp. 5⅜ x 8½. 20610-6 Pa. $8.95

FAIRY AND FOLK TALES OF THE IRISH PEASANTRY, William Butler Yeats (ed.). Treasury of 64 tales from the twilight world of Celtic myth and legend: "The Soul Cages," "The Kildare Pooka," "King O'Toole and his Goose," many more. Introduction and Notes by W. B. Yeats. 352pp. 5⅜ x 8½. 26941-8 Pa. $8.95

BUDDHIST MAHAYANA TEXTS, E. B. Cowell and others (eds.). Superb, accurate translations of basic documents in Mahayana Buddhism, highly important in history of religions. The Buddha-karita of Asvaghosha, Larger Sukhavativyuha, more. 448pp. 5⅜ x 8½. 25552-2 Pa. $12.95

ONE TWO THREE . . . INFINITY: Facts and Speculations of Science, George Gamow. Great physicist's fascinating, readable overview of contemporary science: number theory, relativity, fourth dimension, entropy, genes, atomic structure, much more. 128 illustrations. Index. 352pp. 5⅜ x 8½. 25664-2 Pa. $9.95

EXPERIMENTATION AND MEASUREMENT, W. J. Youden. Introductory manual explains laws of measurement in simple terms and offers tips for achieving accuracy and minimizing errors. Mathematics of measurement, use of instruments, experimenting with machines. 1994 edition. Foreword. Preface. Introduction. Epilogue. Selected Readings. Glossary. Index. Tables and figures. 128pp. 5⅜ x 8½. 40451-X Pa. $6.95

DALÍ ON MODERN ART: The Cuckolds of Antiquated Modern Art, Salvador Dalí. Influential painter skewers modern art and its practitioners. Outrageous evaluations of Picasso, Cézanne, Turner, more. 15 renderings of paintings discussed. 44 calligraphic decorations by Dalí. 96pp. 5⅜ x 8½. (Available in U.S. only.) 29220-7 Pa. $5.95

ANTIQUE PLAYING CARDS: A Pictorial History, Henry René D'Allemagne. Over 900 elaborate, decorative images from rare playing cards (14th–20th centuries): Bacchus, death, dancing dogs, hunting scenes, royal coats of arms, players cheating, much more. 96pp. 9¼ x 12¼. 29265-7 Pa. $12.95

MAKING FURNITURE MASTERPIECES: 30 Projects with Measured Drawings, Franklin H. Gottshall. Step-by-step instructions, illustrations for constructing handsome, useful pieces, among them a Sheraton desk, Chippendale chair, Spanish desk, Queen Anne table and a William and Mary dressing mirror. 224pp. 8⅛ x 11¼. 29338-6 Pa. $16.95

THE FOSSIL BOOK: A Record of Prehistoric Life, Patricia V. Rich et al. Profusely illustrated definitive guide covers everything from single-celled organisms and dinosaurs to birds and mammals and the interplay between climate and man. Over 1,500 illustrations. 760pp. 7½ x 10⅛. 29371-8 Pa. $29.95

Prices subject to change without notice.

Available at your book dealer or write for free catalog to Dept. GI, Dover Publications, Inc., 31 East 2nd St., Mineola, N.Y. 11501. Dover publishes more than 500 books each year on science, elementary and advanced mathematics, biology, music, art, literary history, social sciences and other areas.